The Economic Reformation

A 21st Century Critique of Political Economy: The Way Forward to End the Capitalist Crisis and Restore Economic Liberty, Equality, and Prosperity

Andrew Bodiford

Andrew Bodiford 2023
ISBN:
ISBN-13: 978-1537175171

Acknowledgements

Many thanks to great friends whose conversations have contributed to this book.

- November 13th 2017

Table of Contents

Foreword – 2023

In the time since this book was first written, many new events have accelerated history with significant consequences for the world and its political economy, none more so of course than the corona virus. However, the coming of a revolutionary new AI technology, ChatGPT, could make the story of the last few years an unfinished one. The news as this is being written is filled with stories of Geoffrey Hinton, 'Godfather' of AI, resigning from Google to be able to warn the world of the dangers of advanced technology being misused. He believes the world has seriously misunderstood the potential powers of AI technology. The central question of this book, *who* will be using powerful new technology which is rapidly changing the world and *for what* ends will they be using them, reveals itself to be more relevant than ever.

The virus, of course, has had a huge effect on the world's economic ecosystem. Disruptions during corona virus to the normal supply chain exposed just how complex the world's system for distribution of resources is – a nightmare appearing first with toilet paper, then with big screens.

Not so many years after the financial crisis of 2007, perhaps unsurprisingly, bank failures are back too. As interest rates have risen in response to the pandemic induced inflation, this has laid bare problems in the balance sheets of major banks. This time, it is tech stocks and crypto-currency that proved to be the speculative investment asset creating a bubble – starting with the 2022 implosion of FTX and the saga of Sam Bankman-Fried, of League of Legends in the boardroom legend, and continuing with Silicon Valley Bank, Signature Bank, Credit Suisse, and then First Republic, just taken over at the time of writing by JPMorgan Chase. The more things change the more they stay the same.

Parallel to the analysis this book gives on subjectivity in demand and in finance, the perception of looming trouble at the FTX and then Silicon Valley Bank then combined with the reality of increased interest rates to create classic bank runs. It was perhaps the objective reality that Silicon Valley Bank did not have enough money to pay their uninsured depositors at the bank who wished to withdraw their money for higher interest rates or the perception of safety elsewhere or both that then fixed the outcome. What happened at Silicon Valley Bank did not stay at Silicon Valley Bank. The banks then had no choice but to be saved for the health of the whole financial system, as history repeated itself again.

Of course, Silicon Valley Bank is the same bank that had itself lobbied the United States Federal Government to lower capital requirements when Trump was President of the United States, contributing to its own failure. As interest rates increased, for the first time in decades, stressors appeared in many banks and the next asset bubble bust was born.

Governments thankfully have acted smarter this time. Contagion has not spread nearly as deeply as last time. Anyone who thought this problem was fixed for good was badly mistaken though.

Returning to the impact of new technology today, of course, as we explore in depth later in this book, technology has begun to transform very basic interactions in the economy between producers, their workers, and consumers. Smart AI promises to replace more and more clerical jobs and ChatGPT has only confirmed the trend this book first discussed. The danger, not to humans from AI but to human society by its misuse by the powerful, lies at the heart of the dilemma of AI that we are no closer to solving than before. As Noam Chomsky has pointed out there is nothing truly creative in Chat GPT, but the effects of the blunt computer power to predict human outcomes based on a large data set can be massive for the economy.

Since *The Economic Reformation* was first published in 2016 massive political events have pushed the world towards a fundamental change. This change looks now to be irreversible, just the direction and consequence of the change lie in our hands. Of course, again, the greatest event of this time has been epidemiological, the '*novel*' corona virus, also known as COVID-19. As a natural event and a global disaster it has only further accentuated how for our politics we live in a human civilization that is still inseparable from the natural world.

Much as modern societies would like to create a curated

world set apart from the effects of nature, this nature roared back once again, likely as humans, poetically enough, encroached further into the habitat of a species in the natural world long separated from human civilization – unleashing a new and previously unknown virus pandemic. Civilization strains its necessary relations with the natural world in general today.

This world is a world which still has not taken decisive action against the climate crisis, a failure which increasingly dominates the consciousness of young people everywhere – it is their future which is on the line and their world which faces a threat brought about by two centuries and more of past industry that they had nothing to do with.

The role of technology which *The Economic Reformation* centers on has accelerated the climate crisis even as it has potential instead to be a tool for replacing carbon dioxide emissions. As our productive capacity increased dramatically over the 20th Century since the 1980's, the benefits of technology have enriched the very wealthy, incentives have not changed for extracting oil and gas to profit corporations and the rich for short term wealth, and ordinary people still stand removed from any control over labor saving technology that will transform how the economy functions and goods are made. Employing technology to further the interests of everyone in our political economy is very connected with the challenge of making technology helpful and not harmful in solving the climate crisis. While some progress has been happening there is extraordinary change necessary to redesign our economy and exclude oil, gas, and coal.

The political movements which have been building momentum since 2016 have also shown that there is a huge appetite for change and a powerful clamoring for true equality, though some of it unfortunately appears instead as a narrow minded and destructive nationalist tendency even as the groundwork for real change is being set.

For many people the prospect of this new world conditioned by new technologies and new modes of economic production seems so frightening that an old and seemingly familiar order which in fact never existed becomes worth reestablishing at all costs. This is all a mirage and the reactionary impulse is of course a canard because adaptation to new technological capabilities will be inevitable and technology will change the status quo regardless of what conservative minded people think – the question is just how we should evolve our society to best manage our world. How we respond to change to benefit us all using our collective will enables us to 'take back control.'

There is no 'traditional' way of governance that society would default back to without modernity at any rate and so this idea of restoring an old order is today's greatest neurotic fantasy. Modernity is a permanent wound. Embracing change as an emergent problem is the only way to ever solve our dual crisis and this requires taking a lucid view of the problems which we face without resorting to either reaction or techno-positivist triumphalism.

The status quo is more thoroughly rejected as unsustainable today than it was before, which is its own progress and makes big change possible. Faster than would have clearly been seen in 2016, the 'End of History' seems today in 2023 to be over for good.

The massive structural problems which emerged with globalization since the early 1990's largely unseen by the world's elites are now clearly recognized. Unclear for too many in power though is a way forward as path dependency has set in for many of the managerial classes around the world. Too used to the system as it is, their capacity for creative thought appears limited. They seemingly cannot imagine a world without the 'global economy' as they have known it, though an alternative and truly global economy to benefit the global population is possible, rational, and in some cases even immanent.

The current analysis of the economic crisis of 2007 has not changed dramatically today in light of current events, but in the time since 2016 the mistaken focus on fiscal budgets that drove errors like *Austerity* has shifted.

Governments showed through their response to corona virus in 2020 that they understand that they have an effect on the entire economic ecosystem. The pandemic showed very clearly how interconnected the world's economy is. As well as threatening world demand by shutting down all commerce the corona virus threatened the world's supply by disrupting familiar supply chains.

While the world's industry slowed, an unforeseen magnitude of demand shifted towards an unconventional set of particular goods. The focused demand for manufactured goods not in demand so high previously exacerbated disrupted supply chain and has created shortages and inflation globally as the market failed to respond.

Some people wrongly think that governments overcorrected in response to the recessionary threats of the corona virus pandemic and that this has been what primarily sparked inflation. However, the nature of inflation now and across time is very different than what many imagine and has everything to do with psychological expectations and the origins of resources and true value in the economy. These resources which the world relies on had been both strained and disrupted by changes in the global supply chains caused by the pandemic. Industries were not prepared for these events.

Eventually these strains then may have themselves further strained the familiar landscape of prices around which everyone's expectations structured themselves, unmooring future prices; this set free from these familiar expectations the concentrated wealth of large economic powers to command outrageously high prices that the market before would never have borne, such as for skyrocketing rent as people returned to cities.

Of course, much of the increase in prices also has to do with the original disruptions from the virus which caused shortages in some vital inputs to production, especially as shut downs in factories particularly in China halted normal production. Disruptions in logistics made it more expensive for firms to acquire much of the same basket of goods they had before at the same price. The lack of a response to this disruption in resources and the market failure in ensuring a resilient supply in times of crisis may well have pushed the train out of the station as firms then imposed secondary price increases that they thought people would just have to accept in a world of disrupted supply.

This implicates the role in the economic ecosystem which *objective demand* plays. As the book discusses there really are goods which in a crisis show their value as more than just market 'preferences' because people really need them. These are resources critical for human life in many situations such as food or energy. Many of these resources are the very ones which broken supply chains disordered over the last year particularly after the February 2022 Russian invasion of Ukraine.

These goods *really are* different than demand for hairdressers. This is because they have a different, essential role in the functioning of civilization. By their very nature these goods are more like water in the desert because they have a necessary relation to human beings, often even to human physiology and survival, that is totally different from human relations to other goods – they need to be recognized as such. Political economy demands we take this last step. Their function makes these goods categorically different from others. To accept the human condition in relation to resources the distinction of resources needed for human life is necessary.

In a crisis we see these properties emerge out of the previous ordinary market where these necessary goods may have appeared just like any others at full levels of supply. Governments during the crisis have improvised to ensure that there are continued supplies of food, gas, and industrial inputs in the market as they did in the 1930's and this is a good thing.

Along with these shifts in supply the virus seems to have changed demand at least in the medium term. The problem with demand that existed before still exists though its symptoms have changed since the aftermath of the 2007 crisis as intense demand has begun to focus on certain goods.

The demand for goods has shift dramatically since the beginning of the pandemic. The constraint on people's movements restricted what services people could use, particularly for in person services provided by people through human to human contact. This led to the projected crisis in 2020 about the future of the arts, theater, and public spaces dedicated to human interaction that seemed to lack economic viability during the pandemic. Governments were very right to guarantee the continuation of the economic foundation for the arts and so then these venues returned to normal operations with the return of the people, their customers. Without the vital assistance though that governments gave in recognition of the enormous impact of these services on society, the world's economy after the pandemic might have been much different than it was, for the worse, and there would have been much greater destruction that would have been needlessly inflicted had governments treated the corona virus pandemic like any other in the 'magic of the market.'

The virus also critically put into focus the way we conceptualize time in the economy. Economic activity is structured through a dimension of time and almost all economic activities have some duration or event time. The perception of time that we conceive of in analyzing 'returns' on investment varies a lot over different eras with new conditions emerging after the French Revolution and industrialization; even the notion of economic growth is a very modern phenomenon relying on a modern conception of time that perceives annual growth. Economic growth over a yearly timescale is a product of industrialization, an event which *sped up* time for everything in the economy. Growth in productivity that would have been impossible over one lifetime with a limited level of energy and resources became possible with massive growth rates during industrialization. Industrial production dramatically expanded the economy over the span of one life time starting in the 19th Century so that the world in which people were born into was radically different from the world they grew old in, a change that is peculiar in its extent to this moment in the history of civilization.

Much of the capitalist idea of our growth takes this annualized percentage timescale as its baseline and looks at inputs and disruptions to the system over a short term period. The immense pressure which governments felt at the beginning of the pandemic to "keep the economy open" showed a bias towards this perception which conflicted with the immediate need for action to stop the larger long term damage that the virus inflicted to human health and the economy from serious illness and injuries (even as the world showed that it could maintain workers' basic needs while they were away from work.)

The challenge we have found in combatting climate change derives from the same bias and the same misconception of threats over time that we saw during the corona virus pandemic. We will still struggle with this tension for a long time to come.

The fast paced economic growth spurred by the 20th Century's demand and the quick leaps in the utility of technological change have moved into a period of consolidation when we must structure our world's economy better for what it *should be used for*. Economic goods for human needs should be at the center of our idea of economic utility and efficiency. This by itself would restructure the economic imbalances currently at play in the world's economy and probably spur real, stronger, sustainable growth. We have an incredible amount of wealth and technical sophistication which we could easily use to feed and house the entire world and to provide for healthcare, education and other basic needs for everyone and it should be our social responsibility as to use our wealth for this purpose.

A Foreword to *The Last Crisis* (coming 2024)

We sit at the precipice once again of a very significant change. The world's industry is changing because of AI and automation which brings us a new set of concerns for the people about how these technologies are used – as does of course the coming demand for a new ecological system of energy.

First among the concerns of the people is, surely, how to make a new world of automation and eco-industrialization work for *all* and not just for the few as industrialization has done so many times before. The new industrialization will include industries for the inputs and components in green energy as well as new types of infrastructure for a renewable energy economy. This will create entirely new energy industries that never before existed. Among others, just as one example, this could include a new industry for industrial hydrogen. Of course, new industries will not appear overnight; in the case of hydrogen their development is already in the works though. The effects could have far reaching consequences throughout the whole economy. These are certainly foreseeable changes and have long been discussed. Some of the potential contours of these may well even come to have been predicted a couple of decades ago already in *The Hydrogen Economy*, Jeremy Rifkin's popular book which made a compelling case for hydrogen as the future of energy with many collateral effects for the economy broadly.

Hydrogen is just one example of the countless other potential industries and technologies that will potentially define the next epoch in our economic history.

The change is coming now. Many years have gone by in which the fossil fuel industry has entrenched itself to the detriment to the rest of us who have to face the future of climate change. Now though, it can be said empirically that something is indeed changing as governments have begun to take stronger stands against climate change.

Something much greater still *has to* change. This pace of change will only continue to accelerate with the pace of technology if not because of climate change's demands on humanity alone.

The new industrialization will demand that we amass new combinations of labor and resources than what we have had to have before. It also comes at a time of systemic change; the possibility to reorder the world's economy is not *just* a mere opportunity. Nevertheless, it is also an opportunity out of crisis for us to create a new type of world that will fix many of humanity's problems. In crisis, as it is, there is often opportunity. This is a moment that can transform the economy forever and for the better, if we can take it.

Certainly, before us now there is a painful transition period. The transition will feature political as well as economic change. There comes with this period a yearning for real representation of the people throughout the world today that is pulsing and chafing at the refusal of the powerful to listen or to share power with anyone else, the people having been long denied the proper value of their labor in the capitalist economy. There are also some potential openings for new political paths, again if we can take them.

This is a world of discontent. However, there is also a very paradoxical feeling that people commonly have in the present moment of confusion. At the very center of the potent discontent so many people currently feel can seemingly be located a major disruption of expectations, felt by people as they are thrust into the unfamiliar. The lack of any sense of proximate cause for this can nonetheless create a dangerous situation that can easily spiral into one that ends up making the world much worse for everyone. It is something that makes people upset, and indeed a little crazy for sure.

There are many long term causes that contribute to this discontent. There is a long term cost of living crisis that continually seems to get worse, making every material aspiration more and more out of reach for ordinary people, globally as well as within countries. Greed and corporate monopoly have gone unchecked for decades and they contribute to this discontent as there have come to be fewer checks on the horizontally consolidated firms that raise prices in ways that prejudice everyone in the economy generally. Corporate profits and of course the stock market on the other hand have been fine over this period as a whole extending all the way back to the end of the 2007 housing crisis, despite the shocks of the beginning of the corona virus and then the start of two conflicts which affected commodity prices and contributed to inflation over recent years. The strains of greed and monopoly are concentrated on the shoulders of ordinary people.

The unaffordable price of housing seems to put a decent place to live out of reach for so many, a general cost of living crisis mediated by corporate greed and monopoly seems to have no end, and in the United States the failure of the promise of education weighs on the younger generations with its unsurmountable debt burden of student loans. These seem to be sufficient explanations, generally, for discontent.

The most immediate cause for world disruption is known though and, of course, it is the corona virus. Without this, surely the increased intensity of discontent lately would be hard to explain. The virus' economic impact reverberated through all areas of the economy including, for example, supply chains which has driven inflation; the long term effects are still continuing. However, the aftershocks of this massive event are still little understood even among many of the people as they experience them, many of whom search for a fleeting sense of 'normal' only in vain. This of course opens the world up to the machinations of certain well known rogues who would like to manipulate people's discontent for their own purposes. We have seen plenty of this too. 'Normal,' as people know it, cannot return, at least in the same form as before without a concerted political movement to create the conditions for economic progress and justice that enable a world that is 'normal.'

One very traumatic event – the corona virus – has been the initial catalyst for people to feel utterly dislocated in a way that they have not felt so utterly dislocated in a very long time. The isolation from society and meaningful, purposeful activities in the 'real world' had a psychological impact on the whole world that will take years more to understand. It accelerated a trend that was already occurring in capitalism towards dislocation and communal isolation. This naturally makes people, in a word, mad.

The chaotic present scene stands in front of a backdrop of

what, as we see above, is a much greater period of structural change that is happening. This greater story can interact with people's immediate discontent, but most importantly, it can give us an opportunity to escape it. A new industrialization that can be better than the first ones gives us an out; it is a clean out from this bleak hell that is so commonly painted in popular imagination today in 2024 because it can make real economic change and solve our long term impasse. *We just have to articulate a vision* – which this book will make for a new and prosperous, free and equal world.

Embracing transformation and articulating a vision is the only way out of our current situation – into a new kind of economy. So, here we are. We have to ask some fundamental questions too.

Perhaps the greatest of these for the world today, philosophically, is about what economic value really means in the context of the current need for new types and distributions of resources. *What is value? Why are some things valuable, others not?*

This is accompanied by a parallel, immediate set of questions, *how can we achieve our fundamental human needs* and *what are in fact our fundamental human needs?* These are questions linked to the question of value since they are the questions of *what is the mechanism for how we deliver our needs* and *what do we need?* which is mediated by how we understand economic value.

A necessary third theme of these questions is how we achieve fundamental human needs *for everyone*. We can be assured that the current system does not deliver this, and yet it is what the ordinary people around the world most desperately require. The yearning for our humanity in equality is something that stems from the very most basic desires of humans. This includes more than anything the demand for real human needs. These are the same for everyone - the needs, for example, for food, for shelter, for peaceful conditions for society and love with one another which are common to all humans. These are so universal *for everyone* that we can say that they should be fundamental for co-operation in politics and economics on Earth. Basic human needs are not so hard to deliver with our technology and development. Figuring this out is the ultimate end of our society.

Introduction

"Man is born free but everywhere lies in chains" – Jean Jacques Rousseau

The economist John Maynard Keynes once posited that the purpose of politics was to best combine "economic efficiency, social justice, and political liberty." Keynes' idea of the politics of the economy has hardly ever been better stated.

The word *economics* derives from the Greek word 'oikonomika' referenced by a work ascribed to Aristotle. Oikonomika roughly translates as stewardship or more specifically 'household management' in the particular context of Ancient Greece.[1] This is an important detail. Above any construed economic laws there is a very human end goal of general prosperity in economics – an economy of life. The economy's purpose is to create prosperity, alleviate need, and use resources for the greatest good.

Achieving this end remains an unfulfilled promise of economic reasoning. The actual economy of today strays far from this lofty goal.

The paradox of the world's economy today is that all around we see the signs of progress and great potential for the pace of new science and technology to improve the world. However, despite our great wealth created by centuries of economic and technological progress, material want continues. Despite the vast material resources which the world's people have available to fulfill human needs, the shadow of crisis – both economic and ecological – looms large over societies around the world today.

The destabilizing legacy of the 2007 economic crisis along with its slow, uncertain, and ultimately incomplete recovery and the continuing unsolved crisis of planetary climate change demand a massive global response, an evolution of how the global economy is structured. Change has yet to come; the challenge of the 21st Century has yet to be confronted. The moment of slow moving crisis we face today is a sign that a number of our biggest problems have reached a real point of irresolvability within our current political and economic structures. A great economic reformation is needed to reorient the world's resources. There can be no more putting off the necessary changes that must happen.

Fundamentally the idea of true economy, of *oikonomika*, demands that resources serve human well-being. An economic act should serve to further some goal in the human life process in some rational way and achieving this is how the success of the economy should be judged. Since furthering human well being is the only reason why material goods matter, perhaps in the absence of any sort of religious mandate to make people work and produce goods, it is important that these material goods really do go towards the most important needs of humanity; it is important that they do not exacerbate human suffering.

The trouble today is just how far from this sort of world the current economic system leads us. The world has allowed an economy to emerge that both exacerbates human suffering and also fails to provide for people's basic needs.

With the vast climate change crisis more than anything we have to face the fact capitalism is certainly not doing what is needed in the economy to avoid a looming great disaster yet alone directing goods to the most pressing human needs. Suffering will be wrought by changing climates and rising oceans – this is the reality – but capitalism has failed to adapt.

The vast inequality in capitalism around the world between the people who reap the benefits of progress and those who are not only left out but left behind already suggests that something is very much awry in the economy's design.

If we confront the levels of want that still exist both within countries and around the world in comparison to the amount of growth and production achieved in the last few centuries, we should feel astonished at the failure of the lofty ambitions for progress which economic growth has claimed to further. We live in a very unequal world.

Within the wealthiest countries the benefits of progress from growth, globalization, and technology have gone straight to the richest for the last 30 to 40 years leaving behind the majority of people. To say that the economy's purpose is to serve the greatest good for the greatest number requires that we take this problem seriously.

While growth in some emerging market economies has lifted millions out of poverty, millions more remain impoverished in spite of this vast increase in economic power which these countries' elites still fail to leverage for their benefit. The decline in world growth rates shows that poverty in the global economy will not simply be out-grown. It will not just go away. Poverty is a challenge even many of the richest economies with the most resources cannot seem to solve. In many rich countries it is getting worse – and has been for decades. Even in the most powerful economy in the world, the United States, inequality allows shocking levels of poverty to continue despite vast wealth and resources. Poverty has come to be a political choice. Around the world the reality is that the availability of resources does not intrinsically correspond with the most pressing needs of people – nor does any law, policy, or custom of the 'global economy' explicitly require resources to be responsive to people's most basic needs beyond what unequally distributed money can pay for.

In short our world has an economic system that distributes resources wildly unfairly, generally for the benefit of the richest and most powerful; it is so completely unbalanced it is prone to collapse at regular intervals through financial crisis; even more ominously it has totally failed to deal with the ecological crisis of climate change caused by its own industrial byproducts – primarily carbon dioxide. It can hardly be said, as some might have us think, that inequality, crisis, and climate change are merely the price to be paid for living in a great, advanced civilization.

The economy's inequality, its recurring financial crises, and the ecological crisis it has caused are all stark inefficiencies in the system – seen from the perspective of creating the greatest good for the greatest number of people if not the greatest good for corporate balance sheets. Some economic activity goes to places it should not. Some economic activity does not go where it should and where it is needed. Some very perilous externalities of the economy like climate change are ignored. The scale of this problem demonstrates a stark market failure. No market pressure has yet to solve for it. No political change has yet to make it be solved.

Political complacency is no coincidence at this moment of crisis. To not use the tools we have to envision and create a more rational system is a political choice. It is a choice to not solve for climate change, economic crisis, and inequality – a political act to keep this inefficiency for social utility at the heart of our economic system. This economic inefficiency, disregard for social utility, and failure to solve humanity's great challenges is consciously left in place if not consciously designed.

This irrationality is only explicable because of *who* makes decisions in the economy and *why*. An economic reformation to change the economy's rules is against their interests as much as it is vital for the people and political society and for the future of human civilization. Nowhere does market failure become starker and the political question of how to create a new economy more urgent than with how to distribute the dividends of technological advances.

We live in a time of amazing technological change that will resolve the fate of our current crisis for good or for ill. Technology's great power can go to solve our greatest challenges better than before or it can go to enrich the top tier of owners. Its productive abilities can either help solve for the economic crisis, climate change, and inequality, or it can make these problems far worse depending on how it is owned and used. Technology also accelerates productive power within the existing dysfunctional dynamics of the economy which leads to crisis while creating new dynamics such as automation which deepens its magnitude. Here technology makes the crisis at the heart of the economic system inescapable and our will for how to govern it imperative. What to do with our new technology is the fundamental political question. The decision implicates *who* will have power and what civilization will look like in the 21st Century.

As the economy has evolved modern technology has created new productive capabilities, wrought new dangers like climate change, and enabled new dynamics between buyers and sellers, workers and employers. The economy's old architecture has strained. Structural changes in the economy have often come to the detriment of workers who had won hard fought protections. What was built around old assumptions, of stable companies needing a stable workforce, of stakeholders in a stable marketplace checked by healthy competition, is now an old and dated system as new dynamics have emerged out of new technology and globalization. Old rules of the game no longer work. Companies and the capitalist system no longer respond to the greatest material challenges – economic or ecological – which humanity faces because its architecture is so ill equipped to face the current 21st Century emergent realities. Our system no longer directs our talents, resources, and energies to our greatest needs. What was built for an earlier era – a system to distribute money and economic activity from when the economy was smaller, slower, simpler, more parochial, and less automated, an era with companies more grounded with labor and the societies they were built in, is creaking with our new capabilities. These derive from large productive power that has created significant economies of scale with global trade, financialization, and more than anything new technology.

Technology allows the economy to make more things with less labor. Technology then expands the matrix of economic choices. How this power is realized is our choice in political economy. Technology's expansion of production possibilities presents us with a *great choice*. – one of civilizational magnitude. It is in fact the great choice of the 21st Century. As we see with our planet's delicate ecology this power can both be used for great destruction as well as for great good. Technology can make more things more quickly creating more emissions and it can also produce goods with less labor and emissions. All depends on what wealth society directs new technology to create. The question of what to do with wealth lies at the heart of every modern crisis today. As shall be seen in this book the disruption this new capital creates also engenders the economic causes of human suffering – crisis and inequality. Technology changes the entire picture of economic reality in terms of what is now considered valuable and what is no longer scarce. Making a system that incentivizes technology to be used wisely is most important for this new world since technology can both do more good and create more destruction better than before.

–

The Economic Paradox

The Enlightenment ideals of society guided by reason and humanistic principles now end at the boundary of the economy. While we are born with the same political rights under this paradigm, guided by the ideals of Liberty, Equality, and Fraternity as enshrined in the French Revolution, the basic constitution of the economy remains hopelessly outdated – stuck in its own form of an old régime with arbitrary power stratified in the hands of a few and resources to solve our problems distributed in irrational and inefficient ways.

In the world today so much power has its primary source in *economic domination* by corporations and a rich elite which built up over time, unchecked by society; true social distinction without justification preserves itself here. With command and control of vast concentrated industrial resources which transcend borders, a fact which never existed in the 18th Century, the most powerful have broken free of Adam Smith's paradigm of self-regulating competition. We can imagine this like a poker game. Like the chip leader in poker, the most powerful have amassed sufficient resources to exert control over the game by putting bets into every hand that others cannot afford to consistently call without risking everything, even if they might suspect they have a better hand. The few times the underdog still wins are generally not frequent enough to outweigh the many times the powerful use their chips to end the game before it has even begun.

It is this world in which some proclaim that we should accept the stilted system as it is with its 'winners as winners and losers as losers.' That it is a perfectly efficient system we have that deals with crisis as best as anyone could and that any resulting irrational outcomes or inequalities are justified.

Clearly, this is not so. The inefficiencies in our system – for the climate, for the people – are so massive that it is complete folly to say that this is the best of possible worlds. The form of economic efficiency which our current economics most often appeals to is really a narrow view of short term efficiency for cost from the perspective of the greatest chip leaders. This ignores all the other interests that matter to us as a society – ones which we might want our material resources to efficiently solve. The greatest human needs do not intrinsically have the highest chip values. When considering what is efficient and what is not for the economy the exact efficiency interests involved are key.

Of course, if we are interested in having a system where the best hand most consistently wins, as many capitalist economists insist we should want, this is not it. For justice and efficiency both, there needs to be an alternative to poker games with entrenched corporate chip leaders.[2] Nothing about this system is inevitable. We can change it. Until then we are left in chains to an economy that promised to set us free. What our economy lacks in "economic efficiency, social justice, and political liberty" we need to revitalize, to recreate, to build up from new beginnings if necessary, unafraid to confront follies, irrationalities, and superstitions that pervade its stale orthodoxy.

The prescience of Keynes' formulation is his realization that, at its core, economics is the politics of resources. While we aim to make economic life scientific and rational as much as this is possible, it will always be ideological – as it was made so over centuries by those in power. The economic is political. What fails to function must change. The structure of the economy is a philosophical, ethical, and political question. What does not work well we can fix. We should know from taking a look around the world that, to quote Voltaire, this is far from the "best of all possible worlds."[3]

How We Got Here

Since the Industrial Revolution we have acquired incredible powers now at our disposal. The result of the *economic paradox* is that, as we see, this great power has yielded inequality and continued poverty in all but a few wealthy pockets of a few highly advanced countries, a recent vast (and continuing) great financial crisis, and a looming ecological climate catastrophe in which our supposed economic interests are pitted against the future of the planet.

The recent financial crisis provides a good illustration of the results of our systemic problem. Crisis is itself a product of inefficiency and a large scale market failure. While the market is portrayed as a weird sort of deity which produces all powerful, all beneficent outcomes, natural and inevitable, the best of all possible outcomes self-justified because the market created them, an honest assessment reveals that this could not be further from the truth.

A speculative real estate bubble destabilized conditions in the world's economy after the 2007 financial crisis. Devastating bank failures included Bear Stearns, Lehman Brothers, and Northern Rock.[4]

The travails of the business cycle are presumed to be natural by capitalist economists, yet we have recently witnessed the worst financial crisis in the last 90 years on a scale which few anticipated. There has been an increase in wealth and productivity across the world since then, but this increase has not proportionally reflected itself in wages which the greatest number of people require to live on. Jobs that were always there have been cleared away.

The livelihood of the people whose protection and

well-being are the economy's core responsibility has suffered undoubtedly since the Financial Crisis, if not more broadly over the last 40 years of stagnant incomes for the greater part of people in the developed world. The capitalist economy justifies itself by its own ability to create wealth but it has increasingly failed to do this in a meaningful way that benefits everybody. In this way it is failing its fundamental purpose.

Similarly, beyond these problems of economic distribution and production, the greatest paradox emanating from our systemic problem is that our very own high level of economic productivity is exactly what has also taken a proportionately sharp toll on our climate. Surely humanity does not conceive of the destruction of the climate as just some acceptable cost of doing business, though it may be for some narrow minded owners of industries.

Carbon dioxide levels have risen over 400 parts per million, higher than they have been in millions of years, to which the market has barely reacted at all. The astonishing thing about climate change is that we already knew about it since the late 19th Century when Swedish scientist Svante Arrhenius deduced that fossil fuels could raise the planet's temperature if used widely enough. We knew in particular detail since the middle of the 20th Century what was happening and every United States President since at least Lyndon Johnson had full knowledge of the climate crisis. Since the 1979 Charney Report there has been scientific consensus on the scale and urgency of the problem. The pressure to solve for climate change also reached across all sectors of politics and industry for the next decade before being effectively scuttled.[5] The successful fight to contain the ozone hole through the Montreal Protocol in the 1980's provided a model for how climate change could be fought through international consensus. Margret Thatcher in this era accepted the importance of fighting climate change. Progress was immanent - until polluting industries and pro-business politicians discovered they could fight climate change action.

If there were no trade off for solving climate change then perhaps the market leading corporations would be more inclined to do something, but of course there is a trade off – energy markets as we know them would be completely disrupted through mitigating climate change since oil and gas is largely causing the whole problem and will never be carbon neutral. Fossil fuels continue to burn without any real market pressure to stop them because, for companies, the price of quickly shifting away from them would be too high. Nonetheless what seems too costly and inefficient for these companies is exactly what is most efficient for the interest of society and most necessary for solving our world's biggest long term threat, climate change. The people and nations of the world have yet failed to take decisive action to change this misguided priority of capitalist political economy. If political leaders seem unresponsive, then the market is absolutely brain dead.

There are some examples of people and firms trying to innovate a way out of climate change, but these are exceptions that prove the rule. Tesla captures at most a few percentage points of world market share concentrated in wealthy and socially conscious parts of Norway and California.[6] The vast majority of manufacturers are nowhere close to carbon neutral – and their profits are unlikely to drive social consciousness. We could be potentially confronting the greatest challenge in the history of civilization, not in the least an exaggeration, yet the owners of the greatest economic interests and largest corporations which hold the most power over how the world's resources are used have barely reacted at all.

Remarkably the people who are entrusted with control over the world's resources have been given no incentive to use them responsibly or to help solve the world's biggest problem. Those responsible simply do not have reason to care, invested as they are in the status quo, not the solution. Those who hold the keys to the castle have no reason to defend the cowering people stuck outside the keep.

It is not in the design of the owners of the planet's industries and resources to consider the greater good of people or the planet, even if this greater good is an astronomically important instance of the greater good that affects all of humanity. Economic power under the current structure of incentives discounts the danger of climate change, puts off necessary major changes to the economy, and bargains for half changes that would not threaten prevailing business models. Of course it should come as no surprise that corporations could be selfish, or thoughtless, considering that no greater duty is built into their design and the greater good is not a shareholder.

The structure of corporations does not give them any reciprocal obligations to society in exchange for their legal privileges and ownership stakes over vast resources. This is a result of the deliberate policy choices made throughout history, certainly not just the natural way of doing things.

While the market projects itself as rational, climate change reveals a deep irrationality in our economy that is slowly eating away at civilization. What we suffer from now in all of its manifestations is indeed a *crisis of economic irrationality*. The inability of large corporations to collectively address climate change is symptomatic of their general problem of *perverse incentive*, which affects how they deal with any social problem.[7] Our social institutions, maladapted to the powers of new technology and emergent modern conditions of the 21st Century, fail to incentivize the economic activity most necessary and useful for human social progress while failing to prevent activity that contributes to the greatest existential crisis facing humanity.

Those with the most control over the economy are those least able to rationally manage the current crisis. Of course this is not what is supposed to happen in a capitalist market economy. Markets proclaim their own rationality, their superior ability to determine what the legitimate price to pay for progress really is, and to ascertain the best ways to achieve social good in the economy; however, the market, like any human institution, is forced to make value judgments between conflicting goals. The market fails to properly appraise dangers like ecological crisis when doing so presents a stark conflict with market actors' vested economic interests.

Combating climate change will not be profitable in the near term. It will threaten fortunes. It will be very disruptive to the capitalism of *business as usual*.[8] Those with the most market power to rate the risk of climate change are the very ones whose interests are most threatened. Profit and pollution often dance together.

Financial markets like Wall Street are a democracy of dollars, not individuals, and so whoever has the most dollars invested has the most votes in deciding the outcome. The votes are not evenly distributed; the people and profit do not dance together.

Herein lies the problem. If the market is indeed a forum for self-interested exchange, as Adam Smith believed, and its membership is the sum of its participants and their interests, weighted by their financial stake, its decisions will not reflect the interests of the *greater good* or *democratic values*, but the narrow interests of the most powerful capitalist interests which own the most votes in the market's democracy of dollars. Abandoning a profitable industry, like oil and gas, is not one of these interests, even if it is badly necessary for humanity.[9] If the current capitalist system assumes that those who have the most money also have the most sense, then the world should be very concerned. The beleaguered market system appears overwhelmed in accommodating this crisis it was never designed to solve for – a contingency never thought of by engineers of the 'best of all possible worlds,' indeed a surprise at the 'End of History.' Stopping climate change requires changing how private interests enclose and use resources which strikes too close to the core incentive for production and profit in capitalism for firms to adopt changes independently under the current legal framework. Emergent conditions have created a need to look at factors not built into the system of property before. For decades the political economy of Neo-Liberal capitalism has failed to adapt itself to this glaring problem of climate change. Capitalism is not designed to deal with it. Its architecture is incompatible with solving for it. This is because the problem implicates the whole of modern civilization. Capitalism just will not square this circle on its own in its current constitution.

At some point, in the face of all this evidence that indeed there is something very wrong going on and that the capitalist market will not provide a solution for climate change, we will surely realize that the emperor has no clothes. The only question is whether it will only be too late. Neo-Liberal capitalism asserts itself to be the pinnacle of economic development, something like Voltaire's Panglossian "best of all possible worlds." Far from being the *End of History*, it is instead blindly driving the world towards a precipice, a *dual crisis* of both ecological and financial disaster.

So much of our economic activity amounts to wasted energy that fails to benefit the people of society – in one concrete example our economy's overuse of energy quite literally stems from wasted energy. A recent article published in *Vox* details a little understood problem in our distribution of electricity.[10] It shows through one particular example the challenge the economy struggles with in order to use revolutionary technology in the best ways for humanity.

This development in new technology has revealed that we waste a huge amount of electricity just along the way from the power station to our electronic devices. We use a very dated, inefficient electricity infrastructure. Many instruments used to measure electricity flow have not been changed for decades. Despite being the foundation for almost all modern economic activity electricity infrastructure has gone little noticed in capitalism. However, a revolutionary new technology could optimize the flow of energy and prevent waste if the firm 3DFS is correct. "[I]t could double the energy efficiency of the electricity system, getting twice the energy … out of the same amount of generation. That would hasten both electrification and decarbonization, proving a weapon against climate change at least as potent as renewable energy itself."

This technology is an example of what could possibly represent a generational leap in efficiency to calibrate electricity so that more of it goes to where it is needed instead of being lost along the way. This technology would only be useful though if it is widely implemented. It must be widely used – and shared – but this cannot happen if it is one corporation's jealously guarded proprietary technology. Its promise will go completely unreaped if it ends up locked away at a technology company that just uses it in data centers to save money. The efficiency savings for the whole electricity infrastructure could be massive but because it would mainly benefit the whole society and the end user, not necessarily the distributor of electricity, this does not create the same incentive for the technology's possible owners to spread it. This technology could be revolutionary but only if it is put into use "faster than capitalism would have it."

This is a paradoxical problem its creators foresee. With the wrong incentives in place, where the benefits are too diffuse to capitalize on for the property holder, there just is not much to gain in spreading revolutionary technology. As much as adjusting the economy to combat climate change will inevitably require solving technical problems using new technology it is also about the system and for what ends the economy incentivizes people and firms to use technology.

Currently ownership of intellectual property provides no duty for social utility or the most efficient use of revolutionary new technology even where it could be vital for the future of the planet. The social problem we have is how to create a system which sets us free to use all of the tools we have at our society's disposal to combat its most pressing problems.

In a system where misuse of resources is driven by private owners' perverse incentives, the challenge society faces is how to make profound social utility incentivized. Like other green technology this particular energy infrastructure technology faces the challenge of being all together too disruptive to existing stakeholders' interests and market power for them to enthusiastically adopt it. There is little reason for utilities or energy firms to invest in a technology that would only make obsolete the need for more infrastructure investments which they have sunk costs in. Collective interest is not sufficiently enclosable to guarantee a competitor will take on the established market power hierarchy in an industry with such high barriers to entry either. Like the power system itself with its old outdated infrastructure, the economy can be its own obstacle to maximizing the potential of new technology.

While there may be no explicit law that directs the world to be so mismanaged, it is an *unintended consequence* of the way capitalism functions. Innovation is selectively incentivized when it can provide enclosable benefits. When it cannot do this market power often stands in the way of even the most fundamentally necessary change when the incentives for a profitable status quo to stop change are great enough. These problems are intrinsic to the design of capitalism, a feature not a bug, emanating from the fundamental incentives of capitalism and written into its underlying laws. The fundamental rules are the only avenue through which systemic change to this can come.

There is no single person and certainly no personalized group intentionally directing bad outcomes to happen, as naïve and ignorant conspiracy theories would have it, but instead the mismanaged situation today is an inevitable result of *who* makes decisions in the economy and *why* they make them – as misguided by their *objective* incentives. Too often the wrong people make the wrong decisions. It is properly a political question how to reform the system of political economy and create a system that is responsive to our greatest problems and efficient for our greatest needs and not just corporate interests. How politics deals or fails to deal with this crisis in our political economy will truly determine the direction of civilization and the planet's future.

Our economy today resembles George Orwell's characterization of the British Empire from his 1946 essay "Why I Write," that of "A family with the wrong members in control." Orwell describes a society like "... a rather stuffy Victorian family, with not many black sheep in it but with all the cupboards bursting with skeletons. It has rich relations who have to be kow-towed to and poor relations who are horribly sat upon, and there is a deep conspiracy of silence about the source of the family income. It is a family in which the young are generally thwarted and most of the power is in the hands of irresponsible uncles and bedridden aunts."

The Problem of Emergent Conditions

In previous eras people could only lose their subsistence as a result of some natural phenomenon like a famine or an earthquake or because of something like war caused by the actions of the state or other hostile people in society. The modern world added a new category to the list of things that dispossess people – market failure. Market failure implicates how our civilization misdirects resources leading up to crisis. Market Failure inconveniently interferes with the supposed 'magic of the market' paradigm that lies at the heart of the prevailing economic ideology. This wild factor we have yet to deal with is growing in significance with the complexity of the economy. It is at the heart of irrational decision making that has created both the economic and ecological crisis. As emergent conditions continue to transform the economy through new patterns of business, new technology, and increased economic scale, the destructive potential of market failure only grows. Market failure through the breakdown of the market itself or the inability to weigh the harm of a crisis like climate change is a sign of the failure of the market to self-correct – as it surely would if its mysterious ways were the workings of the 'best of all possible worlds.'

The contradiction in an economic system that features frequent crisis by market failure is that the ultimate goal of economy is of course to remove the conditions of economic need, to abolish itself. The goal of economic development should be to abolish economic need.

In a financial crisis though precisely the opposite happens. The economy generates an artificial income shortage. Artificial need is the result of economic crisis as accounts all over the economy lose assets they previously had, even if there is no real shortage of the critical things people need to survive, things like food or other resources. There was never such a resource shortage in what has become known as the 'Great Recession' nor was there any such shortage in the Great Depression.

No natural or political event is responsible for this artificial shortage. It is a result of a flaw in the economy's design that leads to economic miscalculations. Flawed future projections of infinite growth from illusory speculative profits paradoxically bear responsibility for the coming of many recessions. The preferences of small groups of investors with centralized power over decisions made in the economy cause huge problems when they so thoroughly miscalculate.

The Financial Crisis of 2007-2008 functioned much this way. When so few people with narrow myopic preferences control so much power over the way the world's economy works, which in the era of globalization accounts for truly the *whole world's economy*, and when their scope of control approaches total control with modern computer and robot technology, then there is potential for a very serious problem when something goes wrong. The dangers of 'unknown unknowns' begin to loom large. What Joseph Stiglitz has called the informational problem of markets and what George Soros has called the problem of falsifiability both contribute to conditions for broad market failure at crisis moments that can quickly spread.[11]

Market failure is the market's own self-evident sign that something is not working. Resources are not being directed to where they are most needed.

Emergent conditions demand us to adapt. Emergent conditions often expose previously unappreciated flaws in the economic architecture. They require us to let go of conservative complacency in what we always thought was right and what always seemed to work.

Complexity has in effect killed the self-rectifying efficient market of classical economics. Markets have failed amid the complexity and distortion which modernity has wrought on them and so the necessity of fundamental changes to the economy's paradigm and the rules of the market cannot be avoided. This is partly a critique, partly an examination, and partly a reframing of political economy for the 21st Century. It is not a proposal of any one specific panacea, just an entreaty to ask the really important questions, of which it is our due that economists ask. These questions include how the economy really functions, how the system is changing over time, what the system *should* look like, and what paradigm of economy is really best for the people.

Our economy has ceased to provide the levels of social advancement that it should provide and which it is required to provide to maintain its legitimacy. According to the very function whereby capitalism justifies its existence, the efficient distribution of resources, it is not performing very well.

The problem lies in our underlying philosophy behind economics – the whole paradigm in economics of how markets function, what the role of property is, and what economic agency looks like – is still largely straight out of the 18th Century and out of step with what technology has thrust us into as a matter of reality in the 21st Century. Mistakes in some of our assumptions behind economics which had been minor and harmless are now more serious in the wake of new conditions and new technological capabilities. Some of the biggest ideas in economics have not been properly evaluated in light of modern conditions or consequently updated or revised. We need to drag them kicking and screaming into the 21st Century.

Adam Smith, a product of the Enlightenment, would do no less if confronted with new and modern information about the world. Though Adam Smith would still find the way we look at the very big questions in economics very familiar he would find our world of dazzling technology and scaled up mass production completely novel. In many ways Adam Smith describes a simple and perfect market of fully informed and rational preferences on a level playing field, one which we should be trying to create instead of expecting to appear. Capitalism today consists of many new emergent conditions which Adam Smith did not describe because they did not exist yet. Had he seen conditions of private ownership held by certain groups of firms over key parts of the economy at the expense of the public's need to combat the destruction to the world's climate, and had he seen the lobbying efforts to prevent necessary political change to combat this, a real conspiracy against the public, we know what Adam Smith would say.

Many of the changes to the world's economy are shifting even what classical political economy's idea of comparative advantage looks like since at its heart lies opportunity cost for people and firms which is being upended by automation and new technology. Rationality being the highest virtue, Adam Smith would have adapted to the new reality and what this really meant.

The recent economic recessions are prime examples of the effects of emergent conditions in the economy and the failure of the market paradigm to adapt. During the 2007-2008 financial crisis, a leading British bank employed 4000 risk managers,[12] all of whom somehow missed the big picture that the housing market was over-valued and why that was a problem. None successfully predicted the conditions that would render their bank insolvent and put it under state control. This is paradigmatic of a field of knowledge that is too often allergic to novelty in the scope of its big ideas, despite the fact that the world is constantly evolving and big ideas are subject to challenge as emergent conditions in the economy come about, now more than ever.

These modern emergent conditions are far more relevant to understanding capitalism today than the assumptions which underlaid ideas like Smithian absolute advantage, most relevant to a world where regionally specific goods carried around by 18th Century sailing ships defined world trade – where international trade could only fill the fewer, smaller wooden cargo hulls of ships sailing the seas and specialization of goods across the world arose from sophisticated traditions of craft with origins more complex than just finding the world's cheapest possible labor cost. This was most fitting as the central idea in a different economic reality without the modern technology that makes the world seem so small now – where markets were located far apart from each other instead of at most a 24 hour flight away and conditions of production were markedly different.

The central question of political economy is *who* holds power and *why* – and then what the economy *should* look like. It is a matter of our political choice to change the economic system. Where there is this glaring irrationality at the heart of the system which has not been fixed it is our imperative to change it. This book discusses the ways in which the economy is being disastrously mismanaged in a moment of profound crisis, what needs to be reformed, and the emergent conditions not yet factored into our understanding of the economy from the financial crisis to the present.

Here in this book we will explore particular emergent conditions which are transforming society. These include the evolution of the economy as an ecosystem, the emergence of new technology, and the effects of the law in capitalism. They all three permeate capitalist institutions of markets and property.

As the economy has evolved over time its structure has not adapted with it to meet the demands of novel conditions of today. Structural problems in capitalism today contribute to its recurring bouts of financial crisis. They create its yawning inequalities. They lead to our economy's disastrous inaction on climate change. This results from a chink in the armor of the economic system which had existed harmlessly all along but which has only become more problematic as revealed over the development of capitalism and the advance of technology as the world has changed while the structure of the old armor has stayed the same. The problem is fundamental to capitalism and its structure of incentives and ownership. Most of all it comes from *who* wields power in this system and *why*. This structural inefficiency corrupts the system, our old infrastructure weighing down progress. Productivity is misdirected. A vicious cycle of inefficiency and misallocation of resources results. This entrenches the power of those interests which have been responsible for our growing crisis and our socially suboptimal response to it. Climate change and economic crisis are not dealt with. Inequality worsens.

Shifting economic trends in the economic ecosystem demand change and ensure that the system as it is cannot sustain itself even if it were not creating other forms of social and economic crisis external to itself. This makes technology work less effectively for its fundamental purpose when it enters the economy and then misdirects its benefits to enrich the few. This benefits rent seekers particularly if they can capture the productive capabilities of technology – newfound power which will only perpetuate inequality and poor decision making in an economic system facing crisis.

Technology exacerbates the existing flaws in this

system when it is misused. Technology also changes the fundamental paradigm needed for the economy as the new capabilities of production alter the relationship between different parts of the economic system, the relationship between producers, consumers, workers, and governments. It leaves no alternative to a systemic change. It demands us to respond creatively. The law arises from the expression of society's will which structures the economy of our civilization; because it is in the law where the structure of the economy is created many essential flaws in the system lie here. Emergent conditions and new technology makes adapting the basic law of the economy unavoidable.

In particular, advances in technology produce situations which previous understandings of our economic reality did not foresee. Technology combined with hubris creates a special danger to society. Both the new possibilities and the limits of technology require adaptation. New technology increases our capabilities, but like The Titanic speeding through an icefield on a still April night, the capability of advanced new technology also increases the dangers of miscalculating the risks that lurk below. Unfamiliar realities come with our new capabilities. As our ship gets bigger and faster, and as we are ominously convinced of its own greatness, we risk missing new threats that we never before knew to look for coming faster than we knew to look for them. Technology disorients us. It holds great power to do things never done before while it strips us of the familiar co-ordinates of what we expect machines to be capable of. It warps our understanding of the world to fit the dream of boundless possibilities while there is always the risk that in our minds the perception of this world stays the same as it always was even though it has now completely changed. It is as so today as it was a century ago when The Titanic sailed – presenting us a story of both history and mythology that represents a microcosm of *emergent conditions* involving technology and the modern world at a moment of rapid and disorienting change. The Titanic's air of unsinkability hid the real dangers of speeding through an icefield, of failing to foresee needing enough lifeboats, and, of course, the brutal reality when the ship strikes ice, the unstoppable force of nature which sank the unsinkable ship. To avoid the ice ahead we have to know to look for it coming faster than before.

The truth is our expectations of capitalism must evolve as the world changes. The changes made by these *emergent conditions* of modern capitalism are some of the great changes generally shaping the world – and sharply distinguish it from the world of Adam Smith's *Wealth of Nations* in 1776.

Part I – Dual Crisis & The Economic Ecosystem

Dual Crisis

Crisis struck in 2007. Economists thought they understood the world. While many experts claimed the Alan Greenspan era had solved economic volatility and ensured permanent growth, few with any significant position of power predicted the financial catastrophe that was coming...

The 2007 sub-prime housing bubble saw American house prices rise, at times and places exponentially. During that era many people in the United States made money 'flipping' houses.[1] In red hot real estate markets like Florida people could buy houses and easily double their money. The return was consistent enough to make a career off of house 'flipping' based on nothing more than speculation. United States Treasury Secretary Hank Paulson confidently declared to *Fortune* magazine "This is far and away the strongest global economy I've seen in my business lifetime."[2]

'Flipping' factors into many historical examples of overvalued markets. This was not an unforeseeable anomaly in 2007 considering that the same logic of speculative 'flipping' was at play in the very earliest capitalist commodity bubbles like the Dutch Tulip Bubble. Flowers were traded on a futures market in Amsterdam, each bulb exchanging hands many times each day by investors keen to speculatively re-sell them until the market collapsed in 1637.

Likewise stock price bubbles date back not just to 1929 but further to the South Sea Bubble in the 18th Century and every manner of stock bubbles in the 19th Century like the Panic of 1837 and the Vienna Crash of 1873. This led to the related Panic of 1873 in the United States. It is also well known historically that bubbles like these can have devastating knock-on effects. This series of stock crashes in 1873 triggered a global sell-off that led to the 'Long Depression.'[3] The potential for bubble bursting disaster was well known, historically. These boom and bust cycles are intrinsic to the nature of capitalism.

You can't say we didn't know.

Karl Marx spoke at the time of the coming of 'the great crash' that would apocalyptically wipe out the capitalist class, which would become "its own gravediggers."[4] During the late 19th Century the world was just becoming acclimated to these great crashes in the business cycle. For many it must have seemed apocalyptic. Later as experts became more acquainted with the dynamics of the capitalist business cycle, many leaders attributed it to a passage through a sort of natural life cycle in the economy, while consigning 'great crises' like the Great Depression or the Long Depression to a previous era, the time before we had become acquainted with the science of markets to counteract the unfortunate effects of a business cycle downturn.

The financial crash of 2007 was not fundamentally different from these previous crises, yet it destroyed a certain smug complacency in economics. It was assumed by certain people in certain quarters that such a crash was impossible and would never happen again. Many economists genuinely thought a 1929 Great Depression like event would never happen again – until it did. Our knowledge of what is possible changed forever. Disasters can happen, and they do happen.

A recession widely acknowledged as the worst economic disaster since the Great Depression unfolded as those who had previously claimed to be the priests of economic progress struggled to keep up with the developments. When Queen Elizabeth inquired to the British Academy what exactly had gone wrong during the Financial Crisis, the damning letter they produced declared that "most were convinced that the banks knew what they were doing and believed that the financial wizards had found new and clever ways of managing risks."[5] This is the same Queen's Report in which over 4,000 risk managers who failed to spot the looming financial risk were said to be employed by a single bank that had since been taken into control by the British government. The report continues to say that some of the "best mathematical minds in our country and abroad" failed to see the crisis that was coming, being "most often confined to slices of financial activity" that they "frequently lost sight of the bigger picture."

Seeing how common crashes have been in the past it is hard to believe that so many very intelligent people could have truly not considered the possibility that one could happen again. Perhaps we should pay more attention next time to the insights of historians as well rather than just 'the best mathematical minds' and risk managers.

Most crashes feature similar faulty patterns of thought, as we shall see. In the financialized housing market many people thought that prices could go up indefinitely. Other crashes showed similar beliefs that an investment which had been going up could go up forever, or that what was once a solid investment would always continue to be one. This is perhaps typical of our overall problem of investment not seeing the complete picture – and how it particularly fails to take into account novel long run conditions in the economy.

In a financial crisis, there is an inefficiency at the very zoomed out level of total investment in the economy. The inefficiency could be too many houses being unsustainably financed, or too many goods produced that have no market, or like in the 19th Century too much speculation on railroads. The inefficiency causes the overextended market to fail – such as perhaps with banks whose loans cannot be repaid. There is some mismatch between supply and demand – things going where they are not needed, often going there instead of going to where they would be needed. This initial misallocation ultimately leads to an even greater big picture inefficiency as growth contracts, productive workers remain idle, and investment in useful industries dries up. The inefficiency compounds itself. Many would say this problem is just natural to the business cycle and therefore inevitable. However, it would be mysterianism to say that the reasons for the economy's inefficiency are unknowable because all we have to do is look to know why it is there. To understand this inefficiency requires us to think about *who* makes faulty investment decisions, and *why*.

The Queen's Report tells us *who* was making faulty decisions in the last financial crisis, namely "4,000 risk managers" at one single bank among others working at the behest of banks – certainly a fairly large but narrow cross-section of people. It also gives us a hint at *why*. Clearly these analysts were working for the benefit of their employers the banks. Given that they were only looking at "slices of financial activity" they were likely working to perfect the existing profitable financial model which banks had every reason to want to continue. Considering who they worked for and what their real incentives were risk managers had little reason to question the fundamental model in which they were operating or even to consider its viability. They were not tasked with protecting the system, clients, and homeowners. Not one of the banks held itself responsible for the security of the whole system even though the problem with the whole system in 2007 would eventually bring them to their knees. The perverse incentive structure at financial institutions could conceivably have something to do with why they "lost sight of the big picture." Like the ecological crisis financial crisis has a lot to do with a collective action problem.

Financial crisis is itself really a symptom of an even bigger picture problem in economic decision making that is interrelated with the incentive structure our political economy establishes for people and corporations. So, in other words, follow the money. We can know why supposedly rational actors make inefficient economic decisions from the perspective of the interest of the whole economy. Those *who* are making the faulty decisions are often doing so on behalf of the powerful *because* of a narrow short-term profit interest to do so, even if it contradicts the general interest of society or threatens the long-term health of the economy. In many ways this shows one aspect of a fundamental *conflict of interest* between those who make the most impactful financial investments and society as a whole whose interest it is to have stable investment, sustainable growth, and equitable benefits.

Far from being unknowable alchemy, we can easily understand the reasons why people make economic decisions that lead to disaster. These should not be missed by not seeing the forest from the trees. The fundamental flaw in our political economy which leads powerful actors to disastrous decision making is the way in which resources and decision making are distributed among those responsible only to their narrow interest. This incentivizes important decisions to be made with disregard for the terrible consequences others might face. This is a structural weakness which reveals itself most in economic crisis. It is a problem that plagues the whole economic ecosystem, the whole interrelated system of profits, wages, and consumer spending. This problem is also magnified by the increased possibilities allowed by technology because this enables poor decision making to be centralized and its effects on the rest of the world to be magnified. It contributes to our most obvious economic problems – housing speculation, stock bubbles, the loss of jobs, climate change inaction, and others.

–

The Aftermath

Enlightened expert opinion has yet to completely catch up with this new world because it has so thoroughly shattered their expectations. Economists still fiercely debate what should be done differently now in wake of the financial crisis. Consensus on fundamental basic issues in macro-economics has not been forthcoming, largely for political reasons.

As a result a slow moving disaster has played out over the better part of a decade. In the developed world, asset values plummeted. Stock markets crashed. The Dow Jones in New York lost over 50% of its value from 2007-2009, mirroring the Great Depression. GDP fell, the standard measure for a country's wealth, and it took years to recover across all countries. In the United Kingdom, GDP only recently surpassed its pre-crisis peak. Now in the wake of the Brexit vote, growth continues to be relatively weak while price inflation is up.[6]

In the developing world too, it has increasingly become clear that growth had only been sustained through this period through extensive credit expansion (not unlike what caused the initial crisis in the developed world) that has now emerged as its own form of a bubble. Private real estate investments in China have hit an ongoing crisis point.[7] Chinese growth looks to be permanently slowing down as China no longer boasts of the sort of investment opportunities from the previous decades. Opportunities that had built up over centuries of relative economic decline and neglect in China had fueled supercharged rebound growth as China harnessed its vast resources. Brazilian growth had only been following external growth rates and collapsed following a decline in demand from Brazil's trading partners like China and the collapse of commodity prices for key Brazilian exports. Brazil lies in economic crisis, with a growth decline of -3.8% in 2015, which has spread to include a political crisis.[8] President Dilma Rousseff was impeached, and then removed from office over charges of oil funds corruption at the state oil firm Petrobras that hardly seem credible or unique to her. The better reason Dilma lost legitimacy has to do with the recession and financial crisis, now hitting Latin America. The ultimate consequence, the election of Jair Bolsonaro, is devastating for Brazil and potentially the rest of the world.

All over the world countries that had grown off of credit expansion, high commodity export prices, and trade with booming China now face a reckoning. Russia entered into a period of steep economic decline, with growth rates of up to -4.5% and seven consecutive quarters of contraction, partly because of sanctions, but mostly just because of the low oil price.[9] A return to growth has only come slowly. Russia's entire regime built on high oil prices faces slow-moving crisis. Venezuela similarly has faced disaster from the unplanned for low oil price this decade. For anyone who thinks economic crisis is not global, see the delayed reaction around the world.

Unemployment remained persistently high in most of the developed world in the 2010's, as high over a sustained period throughout the developed world as it has ever been since the 1930's, especially in Southern Europe. With the exception of some countries in Central and Northern Europe like Germany, it still remained high throughout the decade long after markets had recovered from the crash of 2007-2008.

While employment has slowly recovered in some of the developed world, some things have not. Unemployment only slowly decreased after the crash, and often at the expense of lower workforce participation rates and high rates of underemployment. Some aspects of the economy have not been the same since. Underemployment targeting certain social groups remains. Workforce participation rates have been in marked decline in the United States.[10] Unemployment has only decreased in the United States very gradually, despite aggressive efforts at loose monetary policy.

Across the world – at the United States Federal Reserve, Bank of England, Bank of Japan, Svenska Riksbank – unprecedented loose interest rates have been the norm. Real rates are in many cases negative.[11] The European Central Bank has pushed real rates below zero since 2014. Negative interest rates mean banks pay the government to hold its money in securities, and depositors pay the bank to lend out their money after factoring for inflation. This has never before happened over a significant period of time. It is unprecedented in the history of capitalism.[12]

These financial conditions have had a stark impact on society. Youth unemployment is common across the world, and in Southern Europe it has approached 50%.[13] Young people face an inability to find a good paying job, or to use their skills appropriately. In the United States even when they can find a job the value of their work is held down by absurd levels of student debt amassed through tuition fees. Many young Americans feel like they have to attend universities even if they are too expensive to afford without debt so as to have even a chance at attaining a well-qualified position in the economy today. Still many people increasingly work in jobs that they are overqualified for. Advanced academic qualifications no longer guarantee a position. They are necessary but insufficient in many ways to guarantee a role in society today in many areas. Stories abound, admittedly anecdotal, of PhDs working at McDonald's.[14] The gradual economic recovery has still left many people behind. Society has yet to adapt to this situation of under-employment. It is different from what it had previously been habituated to in the capitalist system and there are structural reasons for this.

The Productivity Quandary

There is a crisis of productivity.[15] Taking a step back to consider how this fits broadly with other trends in the economy, part of what contributed to the growth of the original bubble in the first place is really the desire for profit in a market economy because global investors needed a place to put their money which would get solid or better yet superior returns. The profit motive sought the best places to invest money for the highest returns for each individual investor or firm. This combined with insufficient knowledge of what lurked in the details of their investments to create an environment conducive to unnecessary risk. This happens in many bubbles.

By putting money into American mortgage bundles, banks, on behalf of investors, saw appealing returns. This seemed to solve the 'global savings glut' as the Queen's Report acknowledges.[16]

Mortgage bundles with bad mortgages for people with bad credit were deemed to be solvent by credit agencies that gave them AAA ratings. The same happened later with Greek bonds. In the architecture of the European Union and the Eurozone, Greece's debt was seen as failsafe. It was considered to be of equal risk to German debt largely just because they used the same currency, despite the obviously massive differences between the two countries, and so investors hunting for returns piled in to put their money in Greek bonds, attracted to an extra few basis points they would earn over the European average.[17] The rest is history.

It was hardly that the government of Greece offered a unique investment opportunity, but rather that banks believed they were taking advantage of a great gimmick in the architecture of the Eurozone that would give them extra foolproof money for nothing. This mindset could hardly be called economically efficient.

A similar situation is happening with the current slew of bad Chinese real estate investments. These produce the now famous Chinese ghost cities of abandoned buildings and derelict squares of what were supposed to be new boomtowns. Such catastrophic misinvestments at a large enough scale could threaten the continuation of Chinese growth if they continue. While the impact of these investment failures has yet to reach a significant enough level to outweigh the forces that continue to push Chinese growth forward, though at lower rates than before, they still pose a great risk to the future of the Chinese economy. The lesson should be that there is no obvious solution in the capitalist framework to avoid these types of bubbles.

Really, productivity is the thing that technology is changing most dramatically. Productivity expands as technology increases the economy's capabilities. The question of political economy is just how it will be used. This crisis bears witness to the great divergence between what capitalist firms want to do with economic productivity and what the people would do with it instead. The billion dollar bank bailouts in the United States are seared into the minds of many because while banks were saved with state money from failing, the people who suffered most in the recession from the malfeasance of these very banks never got bailed out. The capabilities for the state and capital to invest in the people and build a new economy were vast in wake of the crisis, though this path was never taken despite record low interest rates. More generally though the problem is even bigger.

What the people want and need often diverges from the concerns of capitalist firms. With proper incentives the 'global savings glut' could be used for other purposes, though it suited too many investors to hunt after slightly higher returns guaranteed by an implicit understanding of *privatized profit and socialized risk*. With so much money looking for a home economist Paul Krugman has often suggested for example that the post-crisis economy was the perfect time in the United States for the government to upgrade infrastructure that has been languishing for years.[18] Of course this would have the added benefit of creating new jobs. Many of the new jobs would be in precisely the industries in which employment took a toll after the crash in 2007. Nonetheless this has yet to happen in the face of ideological conservative opposition in Congress.

With the new uses for increased productivity the modern economy has truly created a conflict of interest between the people and the corporations which control the world's resources. The dispute is about what to do with the enormous windfall of productivity and increased technological efficiency that has come with modern industrialized economies. The values and interests of capitalist firms diverge from the legitimate interests of democratic society. In a very broad sense this is the crux of the economic problem we face generally.

With all of the new wealth created by the economy, the people's interests are served by using this to increase equality, reduce working times, and increase the material goods that most directly benefit people's happiness. None of these humanistic goals directly make money for economic interests with the most concentrated power, which of course want to produce and sell more stuff, the profits off of which they can enclose to themselves. The ultimate decision of what to do in our system is left with corporations and those with the most money.

Their bent towards overproduction is not an idle preference. It feeds ecological destruction, created the continuing financial crisis we face now, undermines human well being and resists change.

The real conflict lies in just how to use new capabilities for sustainable growth that benefits human society. Industrial expansion and new technology created new wealth, but this has too often gone up to the very top, and not gone to where new wealth is really needed. It has not gone to solve the most pressing problems humanity faces.

The benefits of growth to people's lives are certainly not always so obvious. While there has been growth over the last 30 years in developed countries, the expected benefits of growth have not followed. Even before the crisis social problems like inequality and industrial job loss in the developed world had already exploded. Growth has benefited large firms greatly. Profits have risen. A proportionate increase in quality of life has not occurred relative to economic growth and capitalist profits though.

As time goes on the rates of growth themselves have recently also not reached the heights previously seen. This is true across the world. If the old promise of growth was enough to ensure 'trickle down' functioned, current 3% global growth rates are not going to sustain this into the future.

–

Financial Crisis – A Historical View

Why so few people saw this crisis coming reflects a persistent attitude among self-declared financial experts. Many of whom did not see that property speculation could lead to a massive crash that could even threaten the liquidity of international banks despite the fact that this has happened countless times before.

There are some strong historical parallels, for example, between the sub-prime crisis in America and the Vienna Crash of 1873. As just one historical example among others, we can see that similar events to the 2007 crisis have happened throughout history and are indeed endemic to our system of political economy. The Great Recession did not happen in a vacuum.

Kaiser Franz Josef of Austria commissioned the Ringstraße as a showplace of Vienna. The new boulevard replaced the torn down city walls that had famously twice defended the city against the armies of the Ottoman Empire. In light of modern firepower, these walls like other types of fixed fortifications had of course become obsolete and without them there opened up prime land for development in the middle of Vienna. This created a huge real estate boom. The subsequent construction of the Ringstraße attracted some of the most famous German architects of the era like Karl Freiherr von Hasenauer and Gottfried Semper, also the designer of the Semperoper in Dresden. The Ringstraße still holds Vienna's most spectacular 19th Century buildings and some of the most amazing architecture of the whole 19th Century like the legendary Staatoper, the Austrian Parliament, the Votivkirche, and of course the Wiener Börse, the new Vienna Stock Exchange building designed by Danish architect Theophil von Hansen that was just being built when the

Vienna Crash happened.

Leading up to this 19th Century financial crash land had been subdivided and sold to new speculators who vied to make money off of this new prime real estate, already the promenade of the city before the walls had been torn down. The construction boom was extraordinary. Many of these new prominent buildings were built by 'Ringstraße Barons' whose speculative real estate investments failed in a huge crash that became known as the Gründerkrach.[19] As investors started losing everything they had in dramatic fashion, the crisis reached even the level of the top echelon of society. Austrian general Baron Ludwig von Gablenz committed suicide the next year, his desperate message for financial support never reaching the Emperor...

We can easily see the parallels today of a huge area of new space opening up for real estate development in the middle of a major global city; without proper consideration the speculation on that land could develop and then, like in 2007, lead to a crash with global consequences potentially spiraling out from it.

The crisis situation soon spread around the world as other investments then began to fail as well. Both Austrian and American investors had put money into redundant railroads which were not particularly profitable and failed under pressure.[20] In the United States failed investments in the Northern Pacific Railroad bankrupted financial firm Jay Cooke and Company and spread panic to other banks. Nothing has really changed.

Too many experts assume that we have a system that is so great, with open markets, with global investment, and advanced technology leading the way; it is so modern, our model so proven, the most efficient way of economic development ever devised in the whole history of the world. In short, they believe this system is the *best of all possible worlds*. This is hubris. Exactly the sorts of things which we thought were so great in the 'global economy' revealed themselves to be key weaknesses which led to the most problems when the financial crisis hit in 2007. Globalized finance first fomented, and then magnified a crisis, which then spread with maximum efficiency through open markets like a plague, infecting city after city. This is the inevitable dark side of a system which claims to leverage benefits off of growth from far away places around the world. We had only imperfect understandings of what direction these trends drove the economy towards. In a globalized world, a crash in New York does not stay confined to New York. This has always been among capitalism's dirty secrets in what has been called the *global* economy, that financial vulnerabilities in capitalism somewhere are vulnerabilities everywhere, and we can see what is happening now as just a repetition of what had already happened countless times in the 19th Century, just with some new details. The Gründerkrach did not stay in Vienna. Finding a solution will require a new global set of rules designed to rein in speculation, laws yet forthcoming.

–

Ecological Crisis

Meanwhile, there is another crisis today. The crisis is a dual crisis. Together with the crisis in economic well being around the world is its twin crisis of ecological catastrophe. Leaders from around the world met in Paris in December of 2015 to debate what to do about impending climate change, as scientists have repeatedly emphasized that the time-frame available to change the course of the planet's warming is precariously tight.[21] If nothing else the climate crisis will force a change to capitalism.

The problem is that carbon dioxide is the refuse from burning fossil fuels which powers the industrial economy. Coal, and then oil and gas have been the fuel used to generate spectacular amounts of energy necessary to power burgeoning factories and technological expansion for two centuries. These fuels are what create greenhouse gas emissions and these emissions are primarily responsible for the crisis of climate change. As a result of climate change, scientific consensus foresees sea level rise that could displace the 40% of the world's population that lives within 100 kilometers of the coast as well as lead to the desertification of mid-latitude climates and the strengthening of super-storms. We are in a dangerous position because the very fuel that powers us has the power to destroy us. The danger we face is that our economy is reaching a zero point where it will not be able to function as it once did without consuming the society that created it because it will be so dependent on energy intensive economic activity while having no alternative to fossil fuels. Many ecologists have even warned that we may have to choose between what we take for granted in modern life and the future of planet and if this continues, a choice we would be loathe to ever have to make.

We can think of energy as a *natural currency*. Energy is what creates action on objects in the natural world according to the laws of physics. Energy and raw materials combine to create manufactured products in the economy. To convert raw materials into finished products requires energy. In physics this energy is measured in joules and while it cannot be created or destroyed, in order to use it for human economic purposes like manufacturing it has to be harnessed. Like the example of electricity described before, the problem with all energy in the economy is how to most effectively and efficiently domesticate it for useful human purposes – industry, transportation, etc. Energy is everywhere, but the economic problem with it has been how best to dam the raging river. The challenge before the Industrial Revolution therefore which we solved with industrialization was not that too little energy existed, but that humans had not yet developed easy ways to harness large amounts of energy. The extraction of fossil fuels changed that.

Since the Industrial Revolution, energy has been too often forgotten and assumed to be a subset or the same thing as *cost*, how much money it requires to perform some economic activity, *efficiency for cost*, which energy efficiency has often been reductively subsumed under without qualification at the grand scale of the economy. It has been naively assumed that energy is an extraneous variable that is either limitless to harness or only worth measuring by its extraction cost at a particular moment in time. In fact energy is completely different. It is constant and independent from fluctuating extraction prices. The physical energy needed to produce power for example is not the same corresponding measurement to the economic cost in currency of pulling coal from the ground or harnessing wind from the air – and the discrepancy between the *physical* economy of energy and the price the economy assigns it to cost is significant for future planning.

The cost of energy reflects many factors including the difficulty of capturing that energy against the demand for energy, in a classical sense of supply and demand. Future supply in the long run and the externalities of using this energy though do not intrinsically factor into this cost.

The physical limits and physical economies of energy are entirely different from the economics behind extracting it. In addition to capitalism's myopic time horizon, the difference stems from the reality that not all energy in the natural world is capable of being easily captured for human industry. Some energy is. However, the economic cost of capturing energy is a changeable reality, particularly with changing technological and social conditions. The types of energy historically easiest to capture are not nature's most prolific or abundant sources of energy nor the most promising future sources. We can compare coal to the sun and think about which one really produces more energy.

This is also what makes for the paradox that fossil fuels are historically the cheapest energy to harness since their energy is stored in a physical object that can be siphoned from the ground and burned, even though their energy represents only a fraction of the energy generated by the sun. Fossil fuels consist of energy bound up in an object. While this tangible object as energy made them an easy early source for humans to harness, burning solid coal or liquid oil creates the ill-fated side effect of carbon emissions.

The cost of energy, classically, should be measured against possible substitute goods and the opportunity cost of the alternatives to buying energy, but this economic calculation is different entirely from the physical limits of energy. Energy therefore should not just be considered another subset of economic supply. It has a critical independent role in human economy. Energy here is a scientific reality from the natural world that can be measured. Its natural properties remain the same no matter what the market conditions and vagaries of demand might be. An inability to harness energy is an *objective* limitation on what can be done in the economy that eventually gets measured in economic cost, but might not be immediately felt if the ease of extraction of energy continues as usual in the short term. Just looking at current cost tells us nothing in itself about the objective conditions of energy then. Much of this is reflected in the market's historical assessment of renewables, not least because the harms of climate change are not an internalized factor in the market price.

Energy failed to be mentioned in classical political economy. Only later was it more fully understood why energy matters, that either there can be a shortage of it, making it a limiting factor in economic activity (like with the possibility of 'peak oil'), more so than other general factors of cost, or that as we know now it can generate dangerous emissions. In economic terms, *energy has no substitute* and for this reason it is unique.

Of course energy is very topical now because releasing energy from fossil fuels creates a highly significant *externality*. This euphemism really just means that *there is an effect on society beyond pure return on investment for the capitalist.*

The side-effect of using fossil fuels is straight forward. Coal causes climate change. This is a big externality. It is a bit like a side-effect of a medicine, except the side-effect of prolonged usage is death. In this instance, the externality of coal, for example, is more relevant than its supposed main function. We can generate energy through renewables now as a substitute for coal, but as of yet we have no way of reliably removing carbon emissions from the atmosphere.

Our industrial economy emerged out of the Earth with fossil fuels like a creation of Dr. Faust. In exchange for incredible power, we have made our Faustian bargain with a force of incredible destruction - and the cost of this deal is measured in carbon dioxide and will be felt in rising sea levels. As we shall see, economic growth and ecological destruction are deeply interrelated so long as we are stuck using fossil fuels. They have moved together in tandem with the advance of industrialization. So long as material production drives economic growth and fossil fuels drive material production, growth and ecological destruction dance together in a deadly embrace.

Before the first trains in Northern England departed from Darlington to Stockton, humans had never before regularly traveled faster than the speed of a galloping horse or a sailing ship. Coal fueled this explosion of power.

Before industrialization, no human endeavor released enough energy to perceptibly change the climate. This new industrial technological universe has upended everything humans traditionally understood about the world. The amount of carbon dioxide created by pre-industrial crafts was proportionally small to the amount of energy they used. This did not amount to very much energy. The new, huge amounts of energy released by industrialization require humans to adjust their mindset to the scale of their own actions. Now with industry consuming massive amounts of energy, the effects of that energy's use are no longer an afterthought. Even these first changes have happened in ways that the human species in human societies has yet to completely comprehend yet alone catch up with.

This situation – of individual firms releasing polluting emissions even though the collective result of these emissions is bad for everyone – is a real *tragedy of the commons*. Private property allocations can be disastrous here given the ownership of goods, but a lack of ownership, and a difficulty in assigning ownership, to the emissions which are a byproduct of making goods. As long as products only get divided out into private property as currently practiced, then there is little restricting the full exploitation of this new property to the detriment of the environment. The market problem is then the incentive for the *privatization of profit and socialization of risk* with a massive threat like climate change.

The more "efficient" and "competitive" this market becomes, the more glaring the problem relating to the shared climate becomes. Firms do not have an incentive with private property to deal with the consequences of emissions on the climate, unless we give them one. There is no way to internalize the externality of carbon emissions or pollution, for example, without some sort of change in the structure of the economy that assigns a sufficient penalty or a form of ownership over emissions that equates to other types of property. The common risk of these problems demands a collective response that creates proper incentives adjusted for the long term risk to everyone.

Climate change poses our most serious challenge since carbon dioxide in the atmosphere causing the problem is imperceptible to most people and the solution, limiting carbon emissions, would severely infringe upon the vested interests of capitalist industry by limiting industrial production which it profits off of. Limiting the use of polluting fossil fuels quickly enough to avert climate change will come at a clear trade off in terms of production costs for capitalist firms.

The sources of carbon emissions are disparate and their effects are devastating, but gradual. It is strongly in the interest of firms to maintain carbon emissions as long as they can, but this threatens the world's future as resistance to necessary changes has delayed global action. We cannot afford to wait much longer, but it is in the interests of firms individually to wait until some external force makes them act on climate change, by which time it may be too late. The economy has to accept change and adopt to the new challenge whether the most powerful like it or not. The ecological crisis demands that we create a political economy responsive to the challenge old political economy was never designed for.

The Economic Ecosystem

What we have witnessed after 2007 is an unprecedented crisis in economic demand which is attested to by the majority of academics in the economics profession. Some have revitalized the Depression Era theory of *secular stagnation* to explain it. [1] The crisis in demand remains long after the financial crisis struck and technology promises to take the existing imbalance in the system and make it worse as it concentrates capital and eliminates unneeded jobs. The crisis in demand both had its roots in long term trends before the financial crisis, but also in the consequences of the financial crisis itself making it the product of a vicious self-reinforcing cycle amplified by recent events.

When so many people in America lost value on their houses, millions went into foreclosure. When some even lost everything they had, it sparked a chain reaction that reverberated around the world. This is precisely what happened after the stock market crash of 1929. It is precisely what has happened in asset bubbles throughout the history of capitalism. However, in 2007 and 2008 people were largely caught off guard, convinced as they were that a 1929 style crash could never happen again.

As homeowners in the United States went into bankruptcy, they no longer had money available to spend on goods and services which lowered incomes throughout the economy. As incomes declined in other industries, layoffs began there as well, starting a disastrous, positively reinforcing vicious cycle of economic decline. Like in the world of the early 20th Century the current world is a globalized world and the crisis which started in the United States did not remain confined there. The economy is an ecosystem. Through the whole ecosystem it spread.

The interconnectedness of the world is both financial – British banks, for example, like Northern Rock held faulty mortgage backed securities in the American real estate market[2] – and general as well. The general interconnectedness of everything is what really made for a global crisis in demand, and not just an isolated financial crisis in America. As demand decreased in America, goods which had been bought in other countries throughout the world, particularly in Europe and Asia, also experienced declines in demand. The recession spread thence to Europe and Asia where major trading partners of the United States went into recession.

Initially the thought was that emerging markets had been unscathed, despite the decreases in demand for Chinese manufactured goods. However, as we are seeing today, knock on effects on the emerging market economies are real; it was simply delayed by the sheer momentum of Chinese growth and revealed itself further by the lowered growth in China and corresponding recession in Brazil and the oil price and sanctions fueled recession in Russia. These have everything to do with lowered Chinese growth, which is a large enough event in itself to alter the aggregate global demand for commodities and the economies of the countries that rely upon them.[3]

As the crisis continues potentially into its emerging Chinese phase, some of the uncomfortable truths of recent growth are being laid bare. The first of which is that growth is just not that high anymore. The World Bank revised its 2019 global growth forecast down once more to 3% after having been between 2% and 3% for much of the decade.[4] Particularly over the last years, the global rate of growth sank as many of the developing countries that had once been doing well entered recession before modestly improving.

The massive effect which China's slowing growth had on growth rates in other countries is another such of these uncomfortable truths. China is so large of a country that its high outlier growth rates over the last few decades had both skewed the global numbers upwards while masking inherent weaknesses. It also created its own economic gravity around which other countries' economies revolved. Chinese growth spurred growth in places that supplied China with raw materials – from Canada to Australia to South America. Even a moderate slowing in China of unbelievably fast 10% growth to around 6% growth has caused a recession in Brazil and a global reduction in demand.[5] Globalization was increasingly just a euphemism for exposure to China's world-historical recovery.

Why is China itself slowing? The better question might be why it was growing so fast in the first place. There are various historical reasons. The most likely answer through for why it is now slowing could be something along the lines of the fact that, first, China is itself not isolated but dependent on trade, particularly with the developed world which it exports to. So when the financial crisis hit the developed world, China upped its own internal investments in infrastructure and real estate but it was only a matter of time before the effects of Chinese industry's customers slowing down also slowed down growth in China, not too much, but just down to a healthy strength instead of a once in many centuries mega-boom, even if that moderate slowing clearly had serious effects for some of China's partners...

This gets to a second reason China may be slowing, a very large scale version of *diminishing marginal utility*. China has come close to recovering its pre-19th Century historical economic strength. No longer are whole areas of China underutilized and its vast population's talents ignored. Chinese factories have dominated many areas of exports manufacturing and there is less room for breakneck expansion than there used to be as this historical process has gone on. It could be that China has just struck against the upper limit of how high sustained growth reasonably looks like. Like the world's other exports leader Germany, it is hard to continue breakneck market share expansion if a country is already on top. As for other countries following the path of China, the Chinese and German export models are not easily exportable themselves because not every country can be the world's largest exporter (even if other countries' exports grew this would probably just come at the expense of the market share of China and Germany and is bounded by global growth). A third reason could be that China is just experiencing a swing in the business cycle. In order to continue growth, Chinese leaders have encouraged a reorientation of growth towards more of a consumer model to reduce its reliance on exports.

The actual causes for rapid global growth outside of China's growth have been few and far between. Other forces sustaining growth since the recession have as it turns out been absolutely anemic.[6] This makes the export driven success of China and Germany even less duplicable for other countries.

As the French economist Thomas Piketty has shown, along with many others, the long term trend of growth is very low by the standards which we are used to from recent history. Just 1% growth signifies massive change over the long-run of generations, and yet this sort of growth rate is considered 'sclerotic' by current commentators. In the late 20th Century, we were used to growth rates of 4% or more per year, which were considered normal, but on the scale given to us by the perspective of world history, 4% growth is incredibly fast.[7] It is perhaps more likely, as Piketty has suggested, that the 20th Century period of supercharged growth is the aberration caused by concurring factors of European post-war rebound and then Chinese recovery from literally centuries of economic nonperformance. Without these special factors contributing to high global growth, conceivably the rate of growth has fallen towards a more natural equilibrium. So perhaps lower global growth is something we have to get used to. Certainly the recent numbers suggest this is possible. Even as the United States and Europe started their recovery from the Great Recession, the global growth rate has been declining to 3% or less, far below what it was at a few decades ago or just before the crisis.[8]

Regardless of its causes, lowered growth and the crisis in demand cause problems. They create a new world which we need to adapt to. While corporate balance sheets have returned to their pre-recessionary figures, growth rates and per capita incomes have stagnated at best.

After the market crash in 2007, academics agreed quickly on the need for a government response.[9] That at least is the general consensus of what happened. Stimulus measures and central bank intervention were made by diverse countries including the United States, Britain, and China. Meanwhile, an entirely different clique of economists argued for even more deregulation and budget cuts in response to the crisis. Soon, this group began to offer its own counter-platform, of what became known as *austerity*.[10] The budget cuts which followed where austerity has prevailed have been devastating for many countries because they have eviscerated vital public welfare spending, destroying the purchasing power of those with the least in society, and they have slashed spending on strategic things like education, health, and infrastructure right when these sorts of investments were needed most, in the middle of a recession when demand was at its lowest and low interest rates gave governments the ability to make once in a generation investments.[11] The *Austerians* and the *Neo-Keynesians* have given completely and totally divergent prescriptions for the economic malaise.

Finance today – for governments – is the ground of dispute between different economics factions as a result. The reason for this reveals much more about a dispute not of economics but of ideology today. On one hand there are those who follow Milton Friedman's economic tradition who espouse the 'supply side' ideas which define the economic philosophy of Neo-Liberalism as a political ideology – the supply side economists almost entirely line up with those whose goals involve furthering a Right-Wing economic platform for political reasons, of economic inequality and larger profits going to a further few. Author Naomi Klein has gone so far as to label this trend *disaster capitalism*, a tendency to use crisis as a tool to extend private capitalist ownership over more areas of society on pretenses that the financial situation requires it, though not really for economic reasons, but for Right-Wing political goals that benefit the wealthy.[12]

On the other side there are the Keynesian economists, who have continued the tradition of the mid-century economists who promoted counter-cyclical fiscal policies in reaction to economic crisis, and who promoted an economic broad base of citizen producers and consumers. Keynesian economists typically line up squarely with the political Left and Centre-Left – the progressive liberals and moderate socialists who championed the unprecedented benefits generated by the welfare state, possibly the greatest in history.

None of this is to say 'pox on both your houses.' Or that these two positions should be held up with some sort of false equivalence. There is a winner – the Keynesians. Economists have shown that there has been a demand problem.[13] Austerity only makes this problem worse.[14]

Austerity has failed where it has been implemented. In Britain, where the Conservative government of David Cameron aggressively promoted budget cuts in the face of economic crisis, economic growth was stagnant and slow in recovery, while targets for reducing British debt have gone wildly missed.[15] The projections were so off that after the British vote to leave the European Union, then Chancellor George Osborne had to abandon the entire enterprise of reducing British debt.[16] Britain's economic performance suffered, tax receipts diminished, and the deficit only grew bigger – to around 90% of GDP.[17] This came after cutting the budget and reducing the deficit had been the cornerstone of British fiscal policy for six years. The entire deficit reduction enterprise is being put in question even by leading Tories.

In Greece, austerity imposed from the outside by German dominated European institutions has had much the same effect – only the disaster has been far more extreme. There has been destruction to basic medical care, education, even state organizations like the coast guard, etc.[18] The budget cuts to public services only eviscerate demand even further while demand is already in crisis, which contracts the economy, which then reduces tax receipts and makes it even more difficult to pay down the debt than it had been before. Greek debt to GDP topped 175% after *austerity* started.[19]

In Kansas where Governor Sam Brownback had promised an economic boom from his supposedly business friendly budget cuts, there was nothing to show for it, except devastated public schools.[20] The outcomes of austerity are painfully obvious.

This is all illustrative of a broader interdependence of different parts of the economy. The economy functions as an ecosystem. Like Adam Smith noted even at the beginning of political economy, what is one person's buyer is the other's seller. The economy is not like one person or one firm's individual budget, but is a web of different budgets.

Being a whole of many connected budgets added together makes it very different than someone's personal finances.[21] If different people's individual finances are the motions of different planets, the economy is a galaxy. It is the health of the overall economy which creates the background conditions for people's personal finances. In personal finance there is a complete distinction between one's own money and someone else's. In an economy it matters how your neighbor is doing. Franklin Roosevelt once said, in a different context, when your neighbor's house is on fire, it makes sense to lend them a hose.

While an individual person can reduce expenditures to pay off their credit card, the economy is a massive web of interconnected activity. One person's expenses are another person's income.[22]

The theories of Austerity treat the economy like it is a giant Lego tower, where 'naughty' governments can just take off extra Legos to 'repay' their creditors if they borrowed a few too many Legos and find themselves with a deficit. However, this is completely wrong. What appears to *Austerity* as a Lego block is really more of a Jenga tower – one miscalculated piece taken away and the entire edifice falls. The economy is a carefully crafted arch; take away the keystone from an arch to 'repay creditors' and the entire arch collapses. The whole cannot then so easily be put back together again.

This is a lose-lose situation for everyone because the people suffer in the ensuing wrecked economy, the government's sovereign debt stays where it is or gets worse, and its creditors never get their money back. The International Monetary Fund has even come around to understanding its own mistake with promoting Austerity.[23] Austerity in this last decade ought to now be recognized for what it is – a politically motivated catastrophe.

Why Is There a Crisis in Demand?

Still though, there is strikingly little in the way of an explanation for *why* there is a crisis in demand in the first place.[24] We will look here at two possible mechanisms for this crisis – the decline in Fordism and a set of processes seen by investor George Soros as 'the mega-bubble.' We will then look at inequality and its effects as generated by economic dysfunction and deliberate policy choices; also we will look the rentier economy which sustains and reproduces inequality and helps maintain the stratified poor decision making behind *who* controls the economy and *why* which contributes so strongly to our political failures to deal with inequality and our dual crisis of market failure and ecological disaster.

The problem with demand is a long-term problem. Factors feeding into the economic crisis of 2007 and the lackluster performance since predated Austerity economics. Some like Paul Krugman and Larry Summers have even speculated that we may even be entering a period of *secular stagnation* where demand is in general retreat, despite all of the policy responses we can come up with.[25] Setting zero-level interest rates while still seeing weak growth does suggest this is possible even if conditions have begun to improve a bit.

Not yet sufficiently considered has been the structural long-term trajectory of economic life throughout the world, and how this has been changing through history with increased scale of production and more advanced technologies. Technology alters the whole pattern of civilization as revolutionary new advances change the whole way we live our lives forever. It changes what people spend money for and how people work and which economically valuable commodities are most scarce. Technology is a clear cause of stress to the economic ecosystem's rigid architecture –

changes which will be explored in detail in the next section. Capitalism structures communities through economic relations. People's lives are imbedded in these economic relations because so much of their lives is tied to their role in economic exchange, of *making ends meet*, so much so that new economic patterns which catastrophically displace some have collateral consequences beyond those immediately impacted. Lost work compounds itself through lost demand but also unpredictably alters the relationships wrought by capitalism into exchange. By upending the long existing arrangements of who buys what, for how much, and whose labor this supports, technology implicates the whole social order.

The answer to why there is a crisis in demand may have something to do with a growing disruption in the economic ecosystem as more forces of disturbance like technology and increased globalization have advanced while countervailing forces of stability in the economic ecosystem have retreated. We will explore here a couple of different perspectives, the decline of 'Fordism' and a financial trend which investor George Soros has ominously called 'the Mega-Bubble.'

Many of the forces which had previously ensured effective economic distribution throughout the whole society have recently weakened over the last few decades, such as 'Fordism' – the model of 20th Century centralized mass production employing vast numbers of people on factory floors. While the decline in Fordism is well understood, some of the implications of it should be more thoroughly explored, particularly as they relate to the fundamental changes which this portends to the political and social compact. The lack of a replacement to Fordism for the Fordist model's labor force is particularly significant for both economics and society.

–

Fordism

Henry Ford understood that the economy is an ecosystem. His development of the assembly line had macro-economic effects by lowering the cost to buy a car for everyone in the economy.[27]

This model of the economy became known as "Fordism." Henry Ford decided to pay his workers $5 a day. This was an astonishing wage at the time, but it was an early insight into the economic ecosystem. While it would seem counter-intuitive from a business perspective to spend this much on labor, Henry Ford purportedly wanted his own workers to be able to buy a Ford themselves, or at the very least he understood that he needed them to stay loyal to his company so that he would have lower costs on turnover.[27] After achieving high profits from a powerful economy of scale, Ford could easily pay his workers more. By paying them at such a rate, he was indirectly helping himself. This is still the logic of a consumer based economy today.

Even if the reward did not come directly to the firm paying higher wages, it would return to the economy and industry generally, driving demand. The wealth of the consumer would drive the wealth of industry. The rising tide then lifts all boats.[28]

Today there is said to be a 'post-Fordist economy.' No longer are there huge factories full of workers driving the economy, at least as much as there used to be. If anything these factories are now highly concentrated in Asia while established firms' high management remains in Europe or North America. Ultimately, the post-Fordist 'service economy' is largely one where manufacturing is still being done, just either in Asia or by advanced technology. As technical capabilities advance it will increasingly be the latter. The presumption of full employment in the economy during good times seems threatened during the current recovery by these new realities – particularly when accounting for underemployment. As we shall see particularly during the recession firms had reasons to economize on labor – permanently. This has wide implications for society. What gets sacrificed in this model are the legions of workers who were needed to run a 'Fordist' factory floor.[29]

As a result of this could secular stagnation suggest as its cause that people are just buying stuff at a lower rate of growth because they have less income? Or perhaps the stuff they are buying fails to trigger growth that it used to since their money now goes to faraway factories with more robots and fewer workers with lower salaries? As the frontier of new markets closes no growth abroad will come to offset any lessened demand. The main culprit could be the collapse of the economic ecosystem's income circulation. This is the flow of resources between consumers, firms, and their workers who consume that sustains all of them. Since every expense is someone's income, more people could just have less money with which to buy less stuff. Demand is a big problem requiring a very big response if this is true.

The economic ecosystem did not first emerge at the beginning of the Fordist economy, since it had always existed, but with Fordism a large tranche of the economy was centralized at an economy of scale in the workings of a few firms. These firms operated at a scale which could influence the economic ecosystem. What lends the name 'Fordism' to 20th Century industrialism featuring mass production, economies of scale, and the assembly line is that highly efficient industrial machines could be concentrated in one firm, Ford Motor Company in this instance. When including the many firms that operated similarly to Ford and existed within Ford's supply chain, this constituted a huge part of the economy. The scale of the firm began to acquire appearances of the state. The centralization of a whole industry and whole economies into the workings of one firm made the performance of this firm and these few firms like it critical to whole regions and entire cities dominated by one massive industry, such as we see clearly with Detroit. These livelihoods of these places then became sensitive to major shocks in employment and production at a few massive firms. The changes in one major industry could shift manufacturing patterns there affecting the whole population.

With Fordist levels of centralization, certain aspects of the economic ecosystem which never mattered before emerged as newly important – none greater than that one person's expenses are another's income. While this created benefits it was a double edged sword because a few major firms could suddenly decide the fate of huge numbers of people. Everyone in these cities and regions would be affected by investment from such a large industry – even those only vicariously connected to it. No small firm could possibly replace the role played by these titans. The dividend of centralization here was economy of scale, but the double edged sword was that this economy of scale from centralization came at the cost of massive vulnerability if anything went wrong. Centralization of economic resources demands accountability and responsible decision making. The stakes become high and irrational decisions are punished severely at such high levels of centralization. The business patterns of a few firms could affect the whole economy.

While in Adam Smith's time no firm could operate at this level of scale without very explicit state support, today the world's largest firms operate at the scale of entire nations. Walmart is such a large corporation, roughly the same size as Denmark.[30] After the advent of Fordism, corporations were no longer only small firms, like the butcher and the baker, but instead rose to the same level of scale as the state.

With individual corporations the size of medium sized countries, a small cohort of firms can determine the fate of the economy of the whole world. None of this changed with post-Fordism. The expansion and consolidation of firms into massive, multinational behemoths has only accelerated as time has gone on, and the economy has become a more 'global' economy. With this much centralization, non-performance at one or a few firms can easily sink an entire economy, while economies of scale allow miscalculated production of goods to exceed demand by mistake or from outside events, causing a general glut affecting prices as in the Great Depression. The change is what happens internally in the innerworkings of these companies and how their activities affect macro-economic conditions like employment and industrial investment.

With the beginning of 'post-Fordist' conditions, centralization did not go away. Firms are just as big as ever. What changed is their relationship with labor and the location and method of manufacturing. Only the scale of the firm's centralized labor force shrank in proportion to its economic weight, at least in the developed world. This still is a shift of monumental consequence. As a result of 'post-Fordism' there is less work than there was before in places where there used to be an abundance of work connected to manufacturing. This has consequences for a whole broader swathe of economic relations.

—

The Mega Bubble

Financier and hedge fund manager George Soros has described the series of events leading up to the 2007 crisis as the 'bursting of the mega bubble.' As he sees it, the current pattern of overleveraged growth based on 1980's style easy money and padded corporate profits has finally hit a brick wall. This model had been unsustainable all along, but the pattern of dominant, but faulty, decision making was repeatedly reinforced by different passing crises which went unresolved.[31] There was a growing gulf on the market between claimed value and real value in asset prices which eventually caused a correction.

The current set of economic bubbles are just the latest in a series of many economic crises which have stretched back for 30 years or more. Irrational decision making of markets hardly constitute a rare occurrence in the current system. Before Lehman Brothers, AIG, or "Fanny and Freddie," there were the Russian and Southeast Asian financial panics of 1997 and the Savings and Loan crisis before that in the '80s. In each case, according to Soros' analysis, the crisis revealed itself as a symptom of a deep, intrinsic flaw in the way that the international capitalist system had been functioning.[32] However, as he sees it, in these earlier crises the original source of the panic, being at the periphery, was eventually dealt with each time and soon forgotten. Without engaging in critical examination, these appeared as weird and isolated one time events unconnected to the broader global economy, and with causes tied to the particular conditions of Russia or Southeast Asia in 1997.

International financial meltdowns like these summoned no critical questions about the underlying economic structure. Solving the crisis, through lowering interest rates and international intervention, appeared to only verify that the system was working, though in fact it was not.[33] Not only was the system not working, but there was a major financial crisis building with each spark which went smothered, like a volcano waiting to erupt, pressure building every year.

A potentially critical flaw for a smooth, efficient, self-correcting market exists in the process market participants go through to understand what is and is not working. Soros details the value of open discourse, not just as a democratic principle, but as a principle for understanding basic truth.[34] Inspired by his mentor, philosopher Karl Popper, he applies the philosophical principle of falsifiability to financial markets in a way few have done in quite the same way and in a way that a wildly successful hedge fund manager like Soros would have the credibility to do. He concludes that there are serious problems...

In the United States, house mortgage debt was the canary in the coalmine for a large problem before the 2007 crisis. It is the illusory zone of financial ambiguity that confuses unrealized capital gains and leverage for demand that often forms the wellspring of financial crisis. The ambiguity lies in whether gains are "real" or not and whether objective fundamentals are driving them. The existence of this level of ambiguity annihilates the claim that economics is merely an objective field of self-regulating prices because prices are never really able to distinguish between 'real' demand and 'unreal' demand caused by financialization, a large part of what fuels growth in a bubble, so long as the market participants themselves have a limited and imperfect understanding of it.

This is the problem. Supply and demand are only the beginning. Markets are not only made up of objective underlying patterns of supply and demand, but also of psychological bents towards one type of investments or another. Moreover, these two interact. The psychological aspect of what will be called here 'subjective demand' influences the very fundamentals of a commodity's valuation. This pattern has been called 'reflexivity' by George Soros in the context of financial markets, and as he contends incisively this insight seriously challenges the efficient markets hypothesis which lies at the cornerstone of dominant theories of finance.[35]

As a result of the pattern of 'reflexivity' which George Soros has described, disturbances in markets not only reflect just the 'animal spirits' of the prevailing mood, but they also change much of the fundamental financial demand.[36] Markets enter into a self-referential positive growth cycle that continues as rising prices reinforce the perception of strength until, as Soros explains, there is a turn where the valuation fails a 'falsifiability' test, inspired by Karl Popper, at which point the price declines as everyone understands it is overvalued.

For Soros there is an interaction between the descriptive 'reality' principle that we would associate with a stock's fundamentals and the 'manipulative' function by which the fundamentals can be influenced by investors motivated by self-interest to make more money and in fact are the ones who decide to what extent a stock is valuable. This could be sort of like the "pump and dump" scheme seen in *The Wolf of Wall Street* or it could be a more systematic pattern of psychologically influenced overvaluation. Thus with the manipulative function the most valuable stock to buy with the most money making potential would not be that of the objectively best company, but the one which is most hyped and best supported by other investors. There is no requirement that this also be the stock of the objectively best company. It could be objectively well run, with a high market capitalization and effective management, or it could not be.

This insight is the same one John Maynard Keynes once had about markets being like a beauty contest – successful products are not the objectively most beautiful goods that win, but the ones which others agree are the most beautiful.[37] Prices are determined by a popular consensus; such consensus is prone to flawed reasoning though and is not unimpeachable because despite this there does exist an underlying objectivity, of real needs, of fundamentals in a stock, that reveals itself over time.

Important to remember, the driving mechanism behind market prices is of money unequally distributed. Far from the pure 'wisdom of the crowd,' the determinations of value are skewed by the pre-existing inequalities in the system which only make it more likely that prices will reflect self-referential interests and psychological bents of those who have money which inflate prices through the 'manipulative function.'

Still prices have subliminal objectivity at the same time that they are determined by subjective consensus. This is no contradiction. It is the result of the assimilation of objective reality back into the limited and subjective perspectives of market participants. Limited perception creates the illusion of a subjective world. Just because humans have a limited ability to *perceive* the universality of the world around them does not mean that objective economic realities do not exist though. If a person lives their whole life in a box, the wider world *outside the box* still exists even if they cannot see it. It is when the shining light from this outside world starts to pierce through the box of subjectivity that crisis happens.

George Soros has effectively described the mega-bubble in the financial system. However, it was hardly just financial. The financial aspect of the crisis was quite literally just the tip of the iceberg – it was the jagged leading edge of a much bigger, broader entity that lurked beneath the waters.

Subjective and Objective Demand

The most complete explanation for tendencies of market demand requires acknowledgment that there is a difference between *subjective* and *objective* demand that expresses itself in the economy. Similar to Soros' idea of the *manipulative function* of speculative purchases inflating real value, subjective demand is demand for goods secondary to the human life process but which genuinely determine a very large part of overall demand by the market in normal conditions. Some economists like those of the Austrian School have argued that all demand is subjective demand. There is a hidden market for objectively useful products that only reveals itself in certain times though, mainly when people do not have enough of them.

Vulnerability arises in this complex open system with inequality. In a crisis people ration what they do not strictly need. Capitalist political economy mixes together subjective and objective demand for goods and both of them are driven by spending and also create people's income through wages in the economic ecosystem but this makes the system more vulnerable to a crisis when people with precarious incomes shift their income towards objective demand – things they need. Other people's income is tied to demand generally, all the things people are buying whether necessary or not, and takes a hit when subjective demand does and cannot quickly adjust. Lost subjective demand affects people's incomes in totally different industries which precipitates a vicious cycle. Objective demand for real human needs affects the usefulness of prices to allocate goods.

Objective demand explains why these certain goods have what economists call 'inelasticity of demand.' These goods, like food, energy, medicine, etc. are things people need, and so they will pay for them even if the price rises. This means that price for these goods is a relatively poor rationing mechanism, and the effect of monopoly command power is relatively strong. Far from being just a random feature of this assortment of goods, these goods show 'inelasticity of demand' exactly *because* there is *objective demand* for them. Objective demand is the explanatory reason for why a price hike will not reduce demand for certain goods. See the famous pharmaceutical markups in the United States from the last few years that have caused an uproar, like with infamous 'pharma-bro' Martin Shkreli, recently convicted in Brooklyn for conspiracy to commit securities fraud and two counts of securities fraud, whose company's AIDS medication Daraprim went up from $13.50 to $750 per pill. (Martin Shkreli is also the jealous holder of Wu-Tang Clan's single copy album "Once Upon a Time in Shaolin;" he threatened to erase Ghostface Killah's parts after being insulted for price gouging AIDS patients).[38]

The Mylan Epipen controversy from the last few years followed a similar trajectory. The price of its Epipen had nearly quintupled since 2010 reaching $608 for a single pack.[39]

Markets can fail here when there is a combination of *objective demand* with stratification of market power with a few owners. Market conditions of monopoly pricing contrast sharply with the possibilities created by technology. Mass production made more efficient by scientific and technical advancements can radically reduce prices.[40] This would be little constrained by any real limits in producing things people need and then distributing them – the thing pricing power in capitalism claims to do.

Consider the 'paradox of water and diamonds' by Adam Smith.[41] The postulates are that water is more valuable for human life than diamonds, but that diamonds are more valuable than water on a marketplace because they are so rare in nature that they have a higher marginal utility for those with scarce supplies of them. This holds true at naturally occurring levels of water and diamonds. Water is very common, and diamonds are naturally very rare. This influences their relative prices as commodities. The wide availability of water across most of the planet makes it cheap despite its critical function, while the scarcity of diamonds makes them very expensive despite their limited use value.

This still does not change the objective utility of water and diamonds though. Their prices are still ephemeral. In a life threatening situation in the desert water's objective necessity would assert itself very quickly while a similar situation that necessitates diamonds would be hard to imagine. Of course we already have the technology to create 'synthetic diamonds' which reduces its marginal utility. If there were a system which produced enough diamonds at scale through the use of a miraculous new technology, it would also break down the paradox since diamonds have limited usefulness and they would be subject to sharply diminishing marginal utility if we were capable of making enough of them.

In reality the paradox of water and diamonds breaks down quickly outside of natural distributions of diamonds, which can be altered through technology. The evanescence of market conditions shows itself in the face of technology. For earlier economists an explosion of diamond supply was a purely theoretical possibility because production levels overall were so low and an explosion in supply inconceivable. Technology has an immense power to destroy old certainties.[42]

The economic scale of mass production breaks down some very old ideas of what is economically useful and what is not. The very basic assumption of economics that people have *unlimited wants* but *limited resources* also breaks down with increased scale of production. It is an illusion, a fallacy rooted in history's lower levels of production efficiency that people have 'unlimited wants.' People cannot possibly want unlimited things because people have a limited amount of time and a limited scope of attention to enjoy what they have.

Of course in the past, when so many of people's wants and needs went unsatisfied, it may well have seemed that their wants and needs for material goods were 'unlimited' – in the sense that 'unlimited' meant 'very big.' Because people do not have an unlimited capacity to enjoy infinitely growing resources, there is a rational limit to people's wants. It may be very high, but one exists nonetheless. Of course, in previous economic eras, nobody would have had any reason to ask where this limit was. This would have been only a theoretical possibility because needs were so high and production levels overall were so low. This world was before modern industrial conditions were capable of creating mass production which could exceed reasonable levels of economic wants.

Capitalism is concerned with the economy being an ever growing pie, and it is assumed that everyone always wants more pie, but at a certain point a rational person would be satisfied because they would approach the physical limits of consumption for a human body over a certain period of time. Their need for more pie is eventually satiated.

The presumptions around limited resources also depend greatly on the current capabilities of technology and should be challenged in certain cases where we should not assume that prices objectively reflect resource limits and instead reflect market power. Some resources like energy are more limited than they appear and others are less limited than they appear.

We should be very skeptical when people say things like "we cannot afford healthcare" which implies a resource limit without considering if one really does exist in our production possibilities or is just being wrongly suggested by the widespread market failure of a corrupt industry. The economic ecosystem's sickness could just as well be artificially setting the high prices. "Medicare for All" in the United States is not an unreasonable demand when looking at the economic need of the healthcare economy holistically and understanding why prices are set where they are and what waste and inefficiency they charge for. Simply assuming prices set for decades by this corrupt industry accurately reflect their economic value is foolish and of course without justification. We have to gain a better understanding of how value in the economy is determined in order to intelligently make judgments involving the distribution of massive amounts of objectively useful resources in the economy.

In reality subjective demand is bounded both by the satisfaction of objective demand for goods necessary for human life and by the limited ability of humans to subjectively enjoy ever increasing material goods – and the opportunity cost which this would impose on the non-material aspect of life, life's love and laughter that have value in themselves and require little or no economic expenditure. Perhaps a natural limit of subjective demand ultimately controls the rate of growth once objective needs are taken care of.

The very basic assumption of economics of unlimited wants breaks down with scale. There is a threshold, a saturation point that may be crossed. Economic growth and economic goods themselves are subject to diminishing marginal utility.

Of course, if something objectively necessary were to

become scarce again, such as water will soon become in some arid places, its objective demand would quickly reassert itself. Pure universally subjective demand of the sort Eugen von Böhm-Bawerk sees[43] is merely an *illusion* created by industrialization's capability for rendering most goods of objective demand commonplace.

There is a need to critique what market prices hold to be valuable and admit the possibility of something unaccounted for leading to the problem in the economic ecosystem – particularly in light of the crisis in demand, new technology, climate change, and inequality. A critical look at market prices outside the box of their self-justification reveals much of both the human condition's needs and the new realities that are created by our technological power.

Of course here lies the contradiction that firms want to have exponential subjective demand growth; then they make more money.[44] This same drive for infinitely expanding growth based off of subjective demand is inevitably exacerbating climate change. As subjective demand reaches closer to a point of contradiction, there is still unfulfilled objective demand in the economy. People still lack food, and water, and health, education, etc.[45] The lack of provision for these things alongside a Crisis in Demand should be damning.

We have great power but, in truth, we misuse it.

–

Inequality

One of the results of the crisis in demand, of lower growth rates, and of capitalism more generally as it currently exists with recent deregulation and lowered taxes on the wealthy and fewer social services is that there is massive inequality. Many people do not have their basic needs fulfilled, while others have billions of dollars. Both objective economic conditions and conscious policy choices have led to inequality, poverty, the breakdown of fair economic distribution, and ultimately what many perceive to be the social contract.

Inequality had been soaring before the beginning of the crisis, and of course, when the crisis struck inequality only shot up even higher across the developed world. Inequality, like ecological imbalance, is a symptom of the disease and a consequence of the design of capitalism today. As pointed out by the Occupy protests in 2011, the top 1% holds more of the world's total wealth than the other 99%.[46] This global oligarchy is staggering. Before the crisis, salaries had been stagnant for the great middle incomes, and after the crisis the downturn got even worse as people in many cases lost their employment and their houses. It is the result of economic crisis and also feeds its continuation. Wealth begets wealth, and poverty begets poverty.

Inequality is a natural result of what results from a build up of wealth at the top and a certain oligarchic and anti-humanist ideology that declares that being poor is only one's own fault and that alleviating poverty should be no priority for society. It also threatens to feed the crisis as people whose incomes have stagnated and declined could starve the economy of its own customers.

Thomas Piketty has given, indirectly, the best explanation of inequality – his idea of r > g or the idea that when return on interest and investments is higher than growth, inequality rises.[47] He shows that inequality has been rising throughout the developed world, and particularly in Anglo-Saxon countries, while at the same time the returns on fixed incomes have increased, approaching 19th Century levels and signaling the return of a rentier class which can effectively live off of the dead money of previous incomes.[48] Keynes' 'euthanasia of the rentier' has been reversed. There is a new class of non-working rich that disappeared to some extent in the mid-20th Century. Many more of the super rich technically do 'work' but have absurd compensation disproportionate to their duties. It follows as a common sense insight that this is *unjust* and probably opposed to social utility because no matter how well a CEO performs, there is no way that they are 500x more productive or harder working than the janitor who works in their building. The percentage of money going to this class has gone up in relation to the amount of new wealth coming from growth.

Piketty has done an exhaustive analysis of tax records in France, as well as around the developed world, particularly also in Britain and the United States. His conclusions are shocking.

His statistics indicate that inequality soared in the 19th Century. This comes as no surprise. We have a collective view of 19th Century inequality, a strong image conjured by the popular imagination of Dickensian scenes of eight year olds working in factories. As Oliver Twist demands "I want some more" at the workhouse it really sears into the imagination the political economy of a whole era. Inequality is what made this image of the 19th Century so poignant. Charles Dickens helped to frame this view of Victorian capitalism in the English speaking world, often so grim and so cruel that it takes much of the lustre off of what was actually in fact the greatest period of growth and technological change in human history *since agriculture*. Trains and the telegraph changed the world much more completely in relative terms than the internet has done today.[49] The 19th Century was truly the period of revolutionary change, of a global economy under the British Empire, and the beginning of the ideal of universal mass democracy after the French Revolution, where nothing stayed the same as it was before, in politics, the economy, or society; it began with the era of Eric Hobsbawn's "Dual Revolution." The paradox of this progress is that people did not benefit in proportion to the level of advancement which was made. Many were left exploited and many were left behind.

What Piketty shows is that in the 20th Century, for various factors that he explains in depth, including the influence of the world wars and the mid-century Social-Democratic consensus, inequality abated. This corresponded with higher rates of growth and lower returns on fixed capital rents. This is when opportunity shone brightest for people who were not born with wealth.[50] The 21st Century now appears to be hurdling towards the 19th Century levels of high inequality, high rent, and low growth amid accelerating technological development.

When growth based income is chocked off rent-seeking comes to replace it, especially when policies that favor the accumulation of capital continue for too long and capital acquires stable and lucrative returns from rent.[51] His evidence demonstrates how the amount of money to be made from rent-seeking has an inverse relationship with the growth rates over the last 200 or so years since industrialization.[52] In times of higher growth the rent seeking economy would not be competitive with the better opportunities available in the growth economy, ones that are also more naturally accessible to everyone and not just those that already have wealth.

The ability to make money off of rent has a strong effect on inequality. Without high growth areas, the amount of inequality in society takes off because people suddenly have no way of reaching self-advancement through new economic opportunities.

Piketty shows this both through the decline in the demographic growth rate (the 'transition') and the decline in the growth of per capita income.[53] The 'meritocracy' as a 20th Century idea depended on its high growth rates. These no longer exist. The reality is that sustained 'meritocracy' is rapidly disappearing.

In effect, *Capital in the 21st Century* is an obituary for meritocracy. What Piketty really warns us about is that we have careened into a system where the benefits of established money outweigh the benefits of talent. Rent seeking promotes the wealth of the inherited classes, who receive money already to invest. Capitalism's supposed social virtues rest strongly on the fading idea of its meritocracy – this idea that people have wealth because they "earned it" and that the method through which this happened somehow embodied those bourgeois, virtues of thrift, work, selling dear, etc.

In reality though capitalism today has become the antithesis of meritocracy. This 20th Century world is gone. Barring some very ambitious and enterprising solutions like the type Piketty proposes, it is not coming back. Instead of people achieving riches through their qualifications and education, like at least in the 20th Century's idealized vision, the wealthy are today able to make vast sums of money by skillfully avoiding taxes in Panama, being well connected to the established business interests, and skillfully riding the waves of speculative bubbles. Poverty presents no immediate concern for these people.

Of course none of this moralism has anything to do with promoting the most efficient distribution of resources. Most of all there is money to be made in rent-seeking – and an opportunity to do it in the current arrangement. Rent seeking thereby then promotes the wealth of the inherited classes who receive money already to invest. The rich pass on their wealth and acquire riches much like any other wealthy person, or 19th Century continental aristocrat for that matter but may prefer to just dress up their gains as something else, while many of the most truly qualified people stay underemployed, their talents never recognized.

The large amounts of 'dead money' per se as during the Victorian Era can have a strong effect this way on the economy today. If someone owns a building and makes a consistent 5% return on investment as Piketty shows is often a normal going rate under current and 19th Century conditions[54] (but not 20th Century conditions), then they are able to make enormous sums of money in the long term without having to invest much 'work' into their enterprise. This of course makes the whole process even more seamless. People who have no wealth already built up cannot benefit from these capital gains as they have no capital to put up for accumulation. For these people, growth is the main way which they have to advance themselves in a capitalist system.

All they have to offer is their labor. As we shall see, with current conditions the value of their labor is in marked decline along with growth. Growth of the 20th Century variety is the one thing which has disappeared most clearly in this current 21st Century world, for various reasons. The common people's means of social advancement in the capitalist economy is being cut off; this ladder to progress is being pulled up and the drawbridge to the castle raised.

Without high growth rates, distribution becomes a very

political topic as the economy tends towards the rich getting richer and the poor having fewer and fewer ways of leaving poverty. The ideas of capitalism and the ideas of democracy come into conflict. In fact, except for in cases of high growth rates like those seen in the mid 20th Century, it can be said that capitalism and democracy have remained in conflict since the end of the French Revolution. The oligarchic distribution of resources in an inegalitarian market capitalism eventually undermines the democratic core of a society and the equality of all which democracy is built on.

In the United States we see the results of this with the controversy over the *Citizen's United* ruling by the Supreme Court which allows corporations to spend unlimited money in support of political candidates, something which many rightfully believe will let those with money distort the political process, which we can assume they will do with an eye in mind to making more money of course. Author of the dissent Justice John Paul Stephens maintained much this same opinion.[55]

Piketty has helped to explain how economic inequality, fostered by deliberate political decisions, evolved over the history of industrialization around the world. After reaching highs in the 19th Century that he explains by his trade off between growth and rent, inequality declined in the 20th Century after the catastrophe of the two world wars. This mid-century golden age, which has been called the 'trente glorieuses' in France, was seen around the world, though in less extreme measures in the English speaking countries which were experiencing less 'catch up' per se from the destruction of the world wars.

Interestingly enough, it is partly the wars themselves which Piketty credits in opening up new space for people to rise through the ranks of society and displace old wealth and stimulate new demand. This is very similar to the pattern of leveling which Medieval historians have shown in 15th Century Western Europe in the wake of the Black Death which partly contributed to new classes of free people in European society.[56]

In Piketty's work, the great disaster of the two world wars takes the place of the Black Death in pushing up the relative value of labor and opening up a previously stilted system to change. After the Second World War in particular, countries around the world enshrined egalitarian policies of Social Democracy that contributed to three decades of fantastic and equitable growth around the world. Inequality declined in the mid-century lull, only to return with Neo-Liberal capitalism in the '80s, bringing back with it many of the features of the 19th Century that had seemed to have disappeared. Whether the 19th Century or the 20th Century came as an aberration is still to be seen, but signs increasingly suggest that it was the 20th Century that was unusual and that there is much from the 19th Century that is coming back to haunt the 21st Century like the great phantom from a gothic novel. There is a spectre haunting the world – the Ghost of the 19th Century Past.

–

Ricardian Rent

The British classical economist David Ricardo first noticed how the distribution of wealth could tend towards the particular class he called 'landlords.'[57] In his time this meant agricultural lords who would rent out their land to farmers while they took the proceeds in rent from the land. As society grew, Ricardo noted that "the rise of rent is always the effect of the increasing wealth of the country"[58] The more workers went to cities, the higher demand for food would be from people no longer working the land. Ricardo's fear was that these agricultural rents could starve the rest of society. Ricardian Rent is what is taken out of the economy for the payment of these 'landlords.' Ricardian Rent returns most strongly in conditions of low growth and high market power for economic chip leaders. Their power over valuable economic assets enables economic distortion which perpetuates crisis and sustains inequality. With their strategic position in control of a necessary resource, food, country lords could divert income towards themselves and away from what David Ricardo (and other economists) considered the most productive and innovative part of the economy – the new factories of the Industrial Revolution that made Britain the richest, most advanced country in the world.

For the liberal British economists of the early 19th Century, it was triumphantly assumed that the repeal of the protectionist Corn Laws would free society from the pernicious influence of landlords. Once opened up to foreign competition they thought that land owners' monopoly power could never sustain itself;[59] this makes sense if the world market is different from the national market, but what if 'corn' were scarce and its price high around the world and not just in one country? Now more efficient agriculture makes this the type of worry that keeps people up at night less.[60]

While David Ricardo interpreted rent seeking in the context of agricultural rent, the same logic applies just as well to different types of 'landlords' who occupy the same position as those of Ricardo's time, including the urban real estate owners we commonly associate today with the word 'landlord.' Housing rent and urban real estate serve the same function today in many cases now as agricultural rent's *ersatz*. It is a highly profitable store of value for landlords. It is simply a new version of the same problem seen before. Under current conditions, it has become scarce. So following supply and demand, it is a valuable commodity. We can see this from the perspective of the landlord. Unlike in the 19th Century or the Middle Ages no real estate tycoon would want to buy up vast land in the English countryside to rent it to farmers. If anything, they would perhaps rent out an old country manor house for tourism. This would probably be relatively more lucrative now than the rent on the agricultural land surrounding it. The relative scarcity of housing is a defining feature of the world today.

We all see this today in our personal experiences. For those who live in New York, San Francisco, or London, nobody has to tell them that 'the rent is too damn high' and growth, reflected in wages, is generally stagnant for those who are not rich; this model of infinite rising rent and stagnant growth can only mean one thing – the depletion of the finances of the common people and sharpened inequality. This heavy blow strikes the standard of living of the middle and working classes and kicks them out of the fortress of their security with consequences across generations.

Henry George, *Progress and Poverty*, and Georgism

Henry George also derived his idea of rent from David Ricardo, writing a half century later in the United States. He compared the plight of ordinary people in London, New York, and San Francisco and he noticed that for people to get ahead, it was easier in New York than in London, and easier in San Francisco than in New York.[61] He attributed this to the value of land. It was a very specific type of land value though which he cited as being important for 'landlords' to control which allowed them to command large amounts of capital and which excluded the ordinary people from society – the pure value of land, minus improvements.[62]

Henry George had an insight that went further than Ricardo's, and which has a lot of prescience today. The theme of his 1879 book *Progress and Poverty* is how a world with so much material wealth could generate such inequality and continued poverty, and the answer he gives is that economic development often drives up the value of land faster than people's wages naturally rise in the market.

This is a paradoxical and highly counter-intuitive result that explains rather well how progress and deepened inequality can coexist. Despite the emancipatory potential of investment in economic innovation to make life easier for everyone, as with railroads in his time for example, it often acts to stratify wealth in practice because with private property a small group of people can assume ownership over the new innovative economic investments which, as a superior product, will take more of the economic pie than the previous obsolete way of doing things which might nevertheless have had a broader set of stakeholders.

Innovation can displace people's existing economic activities without providing an obvious replacement. As those old stakeholders lose their position and the new company increases its share of total economic activity for its revolutionary new product, power and wealth concentrate into fewer hands.[63] The parallels to technological innovation today are obvious. Even in times of great change and economic innovation, in fact especially in times of great change when certain social conditions are in place like ones which we see today, Ricardian rent seekers can amass command over valuable strategic positions in the economy. This perpetuates existing inequalities and market distortions for the benefit of the rentiers. With increasing capabilities of technology the power of some of the strategic positions in the economy appropriated by the powerful has only grown larger and more unassailable.

In this way poverty accompanies progress as long as it encourages the concentration of resources at the very top of the pyramid while undermining the ways by which the top relies on the base. Even if it also increases the size of the overall pie, without a guarantee that new resources would go to everyone this would not guarantee benefits to ordinary people; it might even harm them as it increases the market power of the 'chip leaders' who capture the benefits from new growth to turn the wealth pyramid into an obelisk. Distribution is essential to real economic progress. Without a plan for resources to be distributed across society, a world which looks like this will only remain mired in exclusion.

In many ways the railroads in 19th Century America held a similar place to modern technology companies and advanced manufacturers today, and also held a place of contempt for Henry George. After the railroads came through rural areas of the United States they effectively monopolized the transport of agricultural goods from the Midwestern farms to big city markets. As the best most modern way of transporting goods, railroads were able to charge freight rates which farmers considered exorbitant and which sucked economic power out of rural economies but there was little alternative.

Innovation can create a situation in which there is more wealth overall in society than before, but even less in total (and not just as a percentage) goes to the poor because single interests which control the means of progress can expand their interests more easily at the expense of others – those whose livelihoods relied on the previous stage of development, were tied to the previous economic compact, or could not afford to keep up with the cutting edge of technological development and the higher equilibrium price it puts on resources like land, freight rates for the 19th Century farmer in the United States, or urban rent today. Presumably the more development there is in society the more likely this is capable of happening.

This explains the paradox right in Henry George's title – of *Progress and Poverty*. Hence how as Henry George noticed, the poor were better off in New York than in London, and in San Francisco than in New York, despite the fact that on a level of development in the 19th Century London was ahead of New York, and New York was ahead of San Francisco. Henry George focused on the value of land as the main way in which this happens, but just as Ricardo's principles of agricultural rent can apply as well to urban housing rent today, could the underlying dynamics of land value not also apply to transport rates, or to patents and copyrights held by monopolistic companies? Could the same basic idea not apply generally to manufacturing?

Around the same time Karl Marx pointed out the increased poverty of workers in capitalism even though they were central to capitalist production. This was the basis for

Marx's prediction of proletarian revolution. The precarious position of workers in the new economy under this new type of industrial landlord was a concerning possibility earlier acknowledged by David Ricardo at the end of *The Principles of Political Economy and Taxation*, though thoroughly counter-intuitive for him.

The return of inequality brings with it some of the worst of these 19th Century tendencies which had seemed to have faded away. This results in a very different world from the familiar economic ecosystem of the mid-20th Century. Inequality is reproduced by rent seeking with lower growth rates – and a class of powerful people who have continually made bad decisions for the economy out of their own self-interest while ignoring the most pressing issues facing humanity. This is the *who* and *why* behind the irrationality and perverse incentives in the economy today.

In a lot of ways Henry George's analysis of the economic problem and proposed solution are very similar to Thomas Piketty's today. Henry George's proposed solution of the 'single tax' is a tax strictly on land value, without the value of buildings or improvements. This is the value of land which develops just because of its strategic location. An acre of land in Manhattan is probably a lot more valuable than 50 acres in Manhattan, Kansas and this value is at the heart of the Georgist land value tax. This is not just because there is likely some big building placed on the land in New York. The value of the land itself is higher because people want to rent on that land because of its proximity to economically valuable places.

Location, location, location, is the name of this game. Henry George demonstrated his 'single tax' on land value would be the most efficient, and progressive tax possible, and that it diminishes the power of these 'landlords' who find themselves sitting on valuable locations. It also would be able to replace other taxes and tariffs which he liked considerably less.[64] Location, as seen in Georgism, is similar to other forms of rent seeking based on valuable positions in the economy. Manufacturing based on valuable proprietary processes and technology follows a similar logic as well.

Piketty's conclusion is a proposal for a universal global tax on income from capital. In a lot of ways the principle behind it is similar to Henry George's 'single tax' in that it attempts to tax the proceeds of Ricardianesque 'landlords' who collect rent and returns on their capital. His book is in effect a rigorous defense of the function of Social Democracy. The world of the mid-century, with high growth and equitable distribution of income guaranteed by a high 'confiscatory' tax rate on incomes presents what he argues is the best, easiest solution to our current problems.[65] And he is right.

However, the problem is, as he admits, that these are difficult policies to bring back since they were only created in very special circumstances. The trauma of the two world wars forged the conditions where capitalists were willing to allow confiscatory tax rates largely without objection.[66] Social Democracy triumphed out of the ashes of the world wars. This is because of the large scale destruction of capital in the war and the central place of the working class in the rebuilding afterwards. Now that Neo-Liberal era of Thatcher and Reagan began to dismantle Social Democracy politically, it is hard to unbreak the broken glass.

–

Social Democracy

Piketty admits that it would be almost impossible today to get countries around the world to all agree to the financial transactions tax he proposes.[67] This does not mean that it should not be done or that it is not a good idea. It is.

Its effectiveness would be limited though since firms could partake in shopping by choosing to incorporate in a country without the tax, perhaps Singapore or Ireland. This tax is theoretically sound but of limited effectiveness without a sort of universal implementation which will never happen. As Slavoj Žižek said of Piketty's tax, at the point at which we could implement this tax, our political problem would already have been solved.[68] While economically simple, in a political sense, it is almost utopian.

This line of reasoning is very similar to the realization of Polish economist Michał Kalecki who was an early proponent of what became known as Keynesian policies. As he argued in "Political Aspects of Full Employment," the main weakness in moving forward with these mid-20th Century ideas was that while capital and "so-called 'economic experts' closely connected with banking and industry" would acquiesce to high taxes in the short term in the face of a crisis like the Great Depression or World War II which threatened their profits more than any tax did, in the long run they would put up political resistance to these policies' continuation and push to roll them back.[69] These policies' economic success would be no guarantee of continued political success.

Interestingly as he points out the sort of independence which Social Democracy and full employment gives to labor might be exactly what makes it so objectionable to business as it would fundamentally shift power in the economy, and not just money, away from them and towards the people. Of course from a democratic perspective this is exactly what makes Social Democracy so attractive, but is it any surprise that business interests might not agree? For business, its role as the indispensable node of executive decision making power in the economy is threatened by Social Democracy, which of course would threaten to reduce its political clout as well as its economic influence. Thus, Social Democracy creates a political tension because capitalists whose interests are at directs odds with the well being of the people will chafe at taxes and interventions for full employment. They will resist social intervention which necessarily limits their influence in society, especially their ability to control the people's only source of income without which people cannot live.

Business would eventually try to use its clout to end things like Social Democracy. We have more or less seen exactly this happen throughout the world.

Michał Kalecki suggested that price increases associated with booms would probably be to the disadvantage of rentiers, and that "an alliance of big business and rentiers" not unlike what we really see currently would form to reimpose orthodox 19th Century style economic policy. Of course he was absolutely right and eventually by the 1980's there was enough momentum for capitalist interests to do just what he predicted. Social Democracy, despite its overwhelming success, has been on the defensive for political reasons against the capital's interest to roll back the welfare state. Without a more fundamental change in the economy it was only a matter of time before capitalists seriously resisted "socialist" post-war policies.

In order to get back to the successes of Social Democracy we have to effectively repeat what we accomplished, the creation of the mid-century golden age of equitable growth, but without the devastating catalyst of war to open up society. This can be done. Great transformations have peacefully happened, but it will surely be difficult. It will be a great political challenge for the 21ˢᵗ Century.

Social Democracy's limitation in its traditional form is its source of revenue – it requires capitalism to be functioning well in order to function well itself. By taking taxes out of the capitalist enterprise, it simply redistributes what capitalism is doing effectively, from the perspective of the capital owner. So paradoxically it finds itself in a symbiotic relationship with capitalism. Capitalism requires Social Democracy to act as its stabilizer and engine of consumer demand, while Social Democracy requires capitalist revenues to deliver wealth which it can recover in taxes that go towards its enterprising social goals. This is a problem if in fact capitalism is not doing well, or if capitalist growth rates are lower than they used to be. So we see the dilemma which faced Greece where in fact it was capitalism that fell into crisis, but the effect was that Social Democracy in Greece appeared weak and unsustainable because the economic depression cut into tax revenues used to sustain social services; these were then cut once *Austerity* began its attack in earnest. The capitalist crisis only got worse thereafter because demand got eviscerated which weakened public finances and Social Democracy even further in a horrible vicious cycle.

So long as there is a crisis in capitalism, as this book shows that there is, we cannot simply return to mid-century Social Democracy in its purest sense. We need to traverse a path less travelled. Social Democracy managed well could deal with the market cycle problem but needs to be more ambitious in its scope to deal with all aspects of the problems in the economic ecosystem and needs to have some anchor in physical resources so that it is not too reliant on indirect income from taxation that could succumb to market failure.

Aggressive Social Democracy like Piketty wants and Scandinavian countries effectively have created could in theory manage the system despite the challenges to make adaptations to emergent new conditions. It then becomes a political challenge though to make this happen though.

We do very much need Social Democracy, but we have to create new and better forms of it. It has to find a way to operate independently of the health of the capitalist segment of the economy. Its structure and its income need to be independently grounded enough in the physical resources of society so that it does not lie captive to the fortunes of capitalist business. It needs to be legally established in a way so that capitalist business lobbying cannot easily remove it.

The Georgist 'single' land value tax is an interesting paradigm for this reason. There is a quality to the Georgist land value tax that we should consider more closely for the 21st Century. Like an income tax it could raise revenue to do socially useful things, while acting as a 'confiscatory' tax to limit the power of large concentrations of capital. Unlike an income tax for which revenues vary based on how much money comes in each year and which can be the subject of some creative accounting, Henry George's land value tax is based on the immediately apparent appraised value of land, which the owner cannot haul off to the Cayman Islands. The only way to avoid the tax would be to sell the property. If the Georgist tax is based on the value of strategic location, could the same idea be applied to other areas of ownership over strategic points in the economy to reduce extractive potential from landlord power?

Social Democracy in its many forms, constitutes one of the great achievements of civilization. It is an enduring concept. Its existence will continue to be necessary as long as there are markets prone to distortion. Some form of the "welfare state" will be necessary so long as capitalism functions. Far from Eduard Bernstein's vision of Social Democracy as an evolutionary path to socialism between capitalism and revolutionary Marxism, Social Democracy has paradoxically become an indispensable part of normal capitalism.

This was the main political result of John Maynard Keynes' work though he was a believer in liberal capitalism and may or may not have intended it. 'Socialism' is good for the economy. This is the best possible interpretation of the post-World War II Social Democratic economy that proved so successful (and in a sense why it doomed the Soviet Union 60 years before its ultimate demise – it provided a better product, a better form of Socialism than Soviet 'Really Existing Socialism'). And it is good for the economy. There were special circumstances (such as Fordism) which centralized production within national borders and made these policies more effective, but the basic functions of the welfare state remain very good for the economy. Social welfare distributes money through society into the pockets of consumers and increases aggregate demand which helps correct for natural imbalances in capitalism.

Removing Social Democratic corrections in the market lets free the main distortion in capitalism, the naturally occurring build up of centralized financial capital in firms and the negative effects this has on the greater economy.

The fewer capital's reciprocal obligations to society becomes and the fewer boundaries it finds on itself, the more it is able to indulge its most irrational excesses. In effect, Social Democracy contributes to the health of the economy by intervening against the built-in interference in the market that is inevitable and all but written into the rules of liberal capitalism – monopoly and the build up of centralized private power.

Paradoxically as capitalism has encountered structural problems and lower growth in the last years we have seen increasing demands made to roll back Social Democracy to increase "competitiveness," which has only increased the problems in capitalism by unleashing its main distortion (such as how the erasure of the "Glass-Steagall" rule in the United States, supposedly to increase the profitability of banks, contributed to the effects of the Great Recession of 2007-).

The great irony of the common Centre-Right criticisms of Social Democracy and 'Socialism' is that they are really criticisms of capitalism itself. The shrill refrains against bloated bureaucracy, inefficiency, economic waste, handouts to the undeserved, profligate debt and spending, these are all excellent, valid criticisms of prevailing corporate capitalist culture. They are also very prescient critiques – at least of the structure of corporate organizations. Is a broader degree of sloppy management not precisely what was going on at Lehman Brothers before its bankruptcy? In the Right's typical criticism of the welfare state not just are they are criticizing the institution that likely shields capitalism from a real revolution, but really in the substance of their critique they are unwittingly criticizing the essence of capitalism and its bureaucratic organization in a very direct fundamental sense.

The large scale waste in the corporate model, in office culture, is itself a sign of inefficiency that plagues capitalism in addressing our real, *objective* human needs. This should never be tolerated in a 'real market' except that so many large companies entrench themselves in a comfortable co-existence with each other and face little pressure to take the difficult step of streamlining their bureaucracy unless they find themselves in serious financial trouble. Waste inundates the bureaucratic structure of large enterprises, networks, and whole sectors of vital economic and humanistic organizations such as universities and hospitals. The bureaucratic structures in place are often the simplest for a corporation, even if not the most productive. The top down 'Taylorist' structure is designed to safely streamline large scale profit for corporations.

This criticism applies to some of the great trends of the economy which underlie the organization of capitalist enterprises. Corporate CEOs receive unearned handouts and bloated bureaucracies manage huge and unwieldy companies with thousands of employees who have little say over how their company is run. It is a great act of selection bias to find fault with social welfare while ignoring the huge part of the 'private' economy, guaranteed in its property rights, access to finance, stable legal regime, and political conditions for a market by the institutions of the state, in which waste and fraud are endemic and just part of the culture. Beyond the well reported and debated issue of big bank 'fatcats' getting bailouts from the state whilst everyday people had to foot the bill, these problems are just generally a part of how capitalism works. They are a consequence of the incentives in the current system, the anti-competitive effects of monopolies, the point of diminishing returns they eventually reach, the naturally occurring irrationalities and absurd distribution of resources created by *who* makes decisions in the economy and *why*.

Nonetheless, Social Democracy requires a revitalization to be able to fully take on the dual crisis, the problems in the economic ecosystem, and its effect of rampant inequality. There is no simple answer for how to do this. Some creative thinking is required to come up with new methods and new models to solve the world's problems – some of which are discussed in the last section of this book.

Relativity

A logical principle behind Einstein's Theory of Relativity is that there are certain laws which appear to be universal when looked at from a familiar viewpoint but which no longer describe reality in new conditions never fully considered by science. Newtonian physics works perfectly well in describing motions which are common on Earth at low energy; these could be observed with the technology that predated industrialization. It was the advancement of new industrial powers that enabled the new technology which revealed new facts about the natural world. New technology led to the sorts of experiments which first challenged the long settled view of physics. This new technology of the Industrial Age revealed new behaviors of the physical world that were never before apparent. These revealed a deeper understanding of the true physics of the quantum world which were simply not necessary to know what Newton sought to explain.

Einstein's insight of relativity was theoretically accessible all along, but without the challenge of new and inexplicable modern conditions there would never have been a reason to question the universal validity of standard Newtonian physics.

Albert Einstein of course did not disprove Newtonian physics, he transcended it. He simply stated that within another new category of natural phenomena, *different rules apply* because *different conditions apply*.

While sitting in Bern at the Swiss Patent Office, Einstein developed a paradigm for the *emergent conditions* of physics being revealed by technology. Sir Isaac Newton never imagined what was possible with modern technology and vast amounts of energy.

Relativity's counter-intuitive revelations would have been difficult to predict before Einstein exactly because they only become apparent in special conditions such as high speeds approaching the speed of light. These were hardly fathomable before the new possibilities of industrial technology. Similarly, quantum mechanics, some conclusions of which were considered crazy even by Einstein, only appears crazy because its effects only become significant at infinitesimally small scales like with quarks, a different scale than what we are usually used to.

With the economic ecosystem many of its nuances follow a similar dynamic. The insights Keynes described elucidate how economics behaves differently than with the Smithian butchers and bakers when it reaches a large enough scale – mass production and corporations that reach the size of the state. The Industrial Revolution created emergent conditions which reveal economic dynamics that always existed but were negligible before the advent of mass production and the capture of vast energy.

Climate change was of course happening because of humans for as long as people were keeping cattle and burning wood, but only since industrialization has it been perceptible and significant. The workings of one firm always contributed to market conditions, but only when a firm was centralized and powerful enough like in Fordism did it start to influence the whole market. New technology is starting to alter the most basic interplay between corporations, customers, and workers which would never have received scrutiny before. Like our electricity grid which wastes energy when electronics receive the wrong level of electricity, though we would never have recognized it before we knew to look, our economy is changing and becoming more unbalanced on levels before left unexamined.

That the economy is an ecosystem is not a new concept. It is one though which classical political economy too often neglected.

Technology and techniques of mass production revealed workings of the economic ecosystem which persisted in the background but only gained relevance after the emergent conditions of the modern economy came into existence. Like the Nazca Lines whose true shapes only become visible when flying in an airplane above them, many of the true workings of the economy which have gained new relevance recently are only perceptible when we zoom out far enough to see the bigger picture classical economists never had a reason to look for.

The economic world of Adam Smith's in 1776 when he published *The Wealth of Nations* never considered these factors, not because Adam Smith was terribly wrong in what he saw at the end of the 18th Century, but because the world has changed forever since then.

The world has since been revolutionized. Industry and science have completely reshaped the way everything in our economy is made, not just what happens in a science lab. Gone, forever, are Adam Smith's butcher and baker who can coexist in largely self-regulating competition, never achieving enough monopoly power beyond the capacity of their own productive labor to drive their competition out of business. Gone as well is the dominance of small scale manufacturers whose activities by themselves could never disrupt an entire market. Adam Smith never anticipated the problems of scale created by industrialization. Too many capitalist economists have largely stayed within the conceptual cocoon created by him in many ways though ever since and have been loath to venture out to consider what a Smithian 'conspiracy against the public' might look like today with vast concentrations of unaccountable power now distorting the economic ecosystem.

We cannot live in an industrial world using pre-industrial economic assumptions. Of course many economists would rightfully point out that new economic ideas have developed in response to industrialization, but the problem has to do with the very big picture assumptions which have largely remained unchanged since the 18th Century. Despite the very new dynamics that have been revealed by increased scale in the economy and highly advanced machines which underlie our current crisis, among others the assumption of how participants in a market interact with each other lies largely unchanged. The interdependence of market actors is strongly impacted by emergent conditions in the economic ecosystem and technological innovations held as property by other market actors. As a result we face a situation where the whole architecture of economics has stayed the same and now it is buckling from its inadequate structure as a train hurdling over the trestle of a rotten wooden bridge. Classical political economy treated in economics in centuries before as a universal state of the art model of everything can no longer suffice.

Part II – Technology

Even if we found a way to fix the problems with the economic ecosystem, technology demands that we reinvent the economy. The advance of technology forever upends the intuitive and commonsensical ways in which we understand economic efficiency, the place of work, and the function of market power. Technology and the subsequent increase in productive efficiency change the parameters of what is scarce and therefore considered valuable.

As the world spins, and as conditions change, our paradigm of the world must change with it. Technology is a revolutionary force driving changes in the world today. Over the last years, the effects of technology have been well documented. For example, in a *Vice* article from August 31st 2016, the problem which will be explored here is thoroughly discussed.[1] Many articles published by *The Guardian* have similarly described the looming problem with technology – and particularly the displacement of labor.[2] This has also been thoroughly explored in a 2015 article in *The Atlantic*.[3]

Long considered the Luddite obsession by economists, labor displacement is very real today. All indications are that it functions totally differently now than technological unemployment did in previous cycles of change – and the reason for this is the specific new abilities of technology to change the amount of labor needed in economic production.

Robots, better than previous machines, more completely eliminate the need for workers. This is huge because technology will then be able to disrupt or eliminate the need to pay wage salaried workers. This would also disrupt the cycle of demand in the economic ecosystem described in the first section.

Could it even be technology that is really causing the Crisis in Demand, by eliminating the demand for labor which reduces workers' consumer power? This is an empirical question and there is not sufficient evidence to say here that this is the cause, but this is the logical consequence of labor saving technology, and at some point its logical necessity.

Technology that becomes efficient enough at eliminating labor will at some point necessarily eliminate the laborer, barring massive levels of economic growth, which as we have established is not happening at the current 2% growth rates in developed countries (or even the 6% and declining growth rates in China). Labor saving technology categorically augurs that there should and will be a Crisis in Demand from its increased efficiency after a certain point.

Technology is, plainly, the single greatest catalyst for change of any of the factors of economic production discussed here. Technology is the kernel of the transformation which we see upending conditions of the economy and pushing it past the assumptions in economics underlying what was considered normal economic behavior by 19th Century, or 18th Century standards, or for that matter, even mid 20th Century standards.

Demand and technology of course interact in the labor market. Demand for labor is affected by technological capabilities. This is what has many people worried. Economists who have studied the effects of technology in the economy have come to powerful conclusions. Carl Benedikt Frey has estimated that 47% of jobs in the United States are susceptible to automation – and the number rises to 57% in the OECD, 69% in India, and 77% in China.[4] If this scale of jobs disappeared, the consequences to the prevailing economic model would be catastrophic.

It may seem surprising that such a large number of jobs in China are vulnerable to technological displacement, since

China has been a reservoir of cheap labor which undercuts the cost of manufacturing in the developed world. So far employing a human worker in Asia has often been more cost efficient than using technological automation at its current levels of development for many industries. Technology is progressing quickly though, and it will eventually fill the role that low-paid labor in Asia now occupies. Outsourcing is just the beginning of a great trend towards lower production costs.

As technology becomes more efficient it will eventually get to a point at which it may be cheaper to use a specialized robot to make, say, iPhones, or at least many of the aspects of their manufacture, than to use workers now employed at iPhone factories by Foxconn. Work will also surely go to places with even cheaper labor costs where it can.

For example, there is a new trend, which has been called 'reshoring' in which manufacturing which went to China maybe even decades ago is now coming back to the developed world – but in the form of highly automated, technologically advanced factories. Adidas has announced that it will be moving its production back to Germany from China, but there will be only 160 jobs created because the entire new factory at Ansbach will be automated.[5] In Japan Toyota Motor Company's 'Just in Time' system famously streamlines production and current use of robotic technologies there take automation even further than at factories elsewhere. In labor starved Japan this is hardly problematic, but the ability for factories to operate with a much smaller workforce would be a problem elsewhere. At Tesla's new car manufacturing plants and its new electric car battery 'Gigafactory' near Reno, it promises to use the most advanced technologies for automated and streamlined production and will certainly not feature 20th Century Detroit's scale of workers in the new factory. Henry Ford's model of streamlined, standardized, efficient, 'Fordist' car production has been taken to the next generation, but traditional workers will not feature prominently, except by their elimination.

Even if manufacturing comes back to the developed world, the jobs are not coming back with it. The decline of manufacturing jobs was a permanent change in the economy which we will have to adapt to in the coming decades. Outsourcing was the immediate cause in the developed world, but the same result would have eventually happened anyhow because of technology.

As this trend develops, it will require us to completely rethink the ways in which work, the economy, and some very basic assumptions about our civilization function. The entire way in which civilization is configured will have to change to reflect the new realities of a highly advanced technological world. The possibilities are both great and terrible. The changes that will happen will depend on our ability to socially harness technology in a truly useful and fair way.

To do this we need to transcend some of the firmest self-imposed limits of our economic imagination and envision what a new world defined by great technological power and massive industrial efficiency could be like. We need to dream bigger and look beyond the imagined *End of History*. Our twin ecological dilemma demands that we use technology thoughtfully and appropriately anyhow, lest we succumb to a very different end of history – of a global environmental catastrophe; we have so far failed to resist the temptation of using highly efficient technology to fuel overproduction for increased profit, which of course consumes resources and expels carbon into the atmosphere. We can choose how technology will be harnessed for the benefit of humanity.

–

Technological Reckoning

It is clear that recent events are not simply a matter of 'de-coupling' between the Third World emerging economies and the supposedly 'sclerotic' First World ones. What started in the developed world will slowly reverberate everywhere. China's jobs too will necessarily be undercut by automation once it reaches a certain point of cost effectiveness.

Technology which cannot be unlearnt permanently changes the stoichiometry of inputs for production which alters the social fabric for supplying them just like agriculture, the horse, and the Industrial Revolution did before. Technological innovations enable factories to harness greater amounts of energy and use them more efficiently towards human economic goals. The obvious advantages of this new material system will eventually overwhelm and outcompete previous ways of doing things – all over the world.

To be clear, these predictions about technology's coming role of displacement in the economy are not some fringe view. They are not just something out of science fiction. Technology in the economy is changing the world right now. Just in 2016, Klaus Schwab, founder of the World Economic Forum published a book called *The Fourth Industrial Revolution* in which he details the results of new technologies of the ubiquitous internet, artificial intelligence, advanced robotics, 3D printing, and new biotechnology among others.[6]

One of the facts he quickly points out is that while the three biggest Silicon Valley technology firms in 2014 had a market capitalization 3x higher than the "Big Three" American automakers in Detroit had in 1990, they employed 10x *fewer* workers.

This means high technology companies, the supposed 'vanguard' of the new economy, will actually require 30x fewer workers per unit of capital than the old car companies did. No reasonable amount of future growth could make up for this decline in labor demand.

The effects which new technologies of automation will have on workers will be huge. Many of the most futuristic sounding changes which will come about soon as a result of advanced technology he lists as "Tipping Points" together with their statistical probability– for example he gives an 85.5% chance that 10% of reading glasses will be connected to the internet by 2025. He gathers this information from a 2015 World Economic Forum source *Deep Shift – Technology Tipping Points and Societal Impact*. Klaus Schwab is fully cognizant of the challenge this new world presents and fully admits "... we must embark on restructuring our economic, social and political systems to take full advantage of the opportunities presented... This will clearly require systemic innovation and not small-scale adjustments or reforms at the margin." The theme of the 2016 World Economic Forum meeting at Davos was "mastering the fourth industrial revolution."

Rise of the Robots is the title of another recent book by Martin Ford in which he describes in detail the specific effects of robots, artificial intelligence, and automation, and how this will radically change the world we live in.[7] Martin Ford details many of the innovations which are advancing faster than people realize, such as highly intelligent artificial intelligence like IBM's *Watson* which beat Ken Jennings at *Jeopardy* and can be easily applied to other fields. Computers can now drive cars, write legal documents, and even compose music.

Easily duplicable economic goods newly created by technology will also wreck classical comparative advantage and absolute advantage because these rely on an economic actor's opportunity cost. This is the idea that one person, no matter how talented, cannot do so many things at once and will have to trade for someone else's labor to do what they are least good at – technology today though can easily learn, duplicate, and improve a person's talents and extend their capabilities. This greatly removes this economic limitation, the need for the sort of 'spare labor' that is assumed by Smithian economics. Increased technological efficiency eliminates the trade-offs for time assumed by classical economists.

We just have to see the wreckage which digital media wrought on the record and movie industries to recognize some very real effects technology has already had. This could be seen as a template of what will come later, perhaps with AI and 3D printing. Music and movies can almost instantly and effortlessly be accessed on a computer thanks to new ways of downloading and streaming them. This consumes only a minimal cost measured in computer storage, power, and streaming speed. Old media companies are being eviscerated, despite some of their desperate rearguard attempts to artificially protect their businesses with copyright law.[8]

Underpinning the classical concept of absolute advantage in trade is a commonsensical assumption from the 18th Century about time – that an economic actor's productive efficiency is bounded by time constraints. There are, of course, only 24 hours in a day. No person can work more hours in a day than that no matter how ambitiously productive. Time is very much still a limit on what humans can do but with higher levels of technology it is increasingly not a limit on what human industry can produce since production can happen independent of human input. A product of Silicon Valley himself, Martin Ford predicts without any false sense of optimism that the situation with robots replacing human jobs could become severe enough if mishandled that almost all jobs are replaced, which could eviscerate demand and wreck the economy.

Paradoxically, in an economy based on exchange, if one factor becomes too efficient it can destroy the functioning of the broader economic ecosystem, as we have seen. Time, scale, and duplicability are all aspects of economic production which modern technologies have been changing in ways that make 18th Century assumptions about the way the world works obsolete. A bargain for exchange loses its value when one side loses all bargaining power.

Absolute advantage will be no protection against technologies that increase productive efficiency while also eliminating time constraints that used to limit human productivity in economic production, as computers and automated production technology do. This will inevitably skew markets in ways that benefit capital owners and punish those who only have their labor to offer.

Martin Ford ruthlessly takes out many of the comforting illusions which many people hold on to about automation, such as the idea that people with education will be fine. He suggests there are actually *diminishing returns to education* as a way of building skills which will become more obvious as more and more people obtain degrees. Even in universities, the most education dependent careers, automation promises to change the economics of learning through artificial intelligence powered grading technology which would replace unnecessary teaching assistants.

In *The Second Machine Age* Brynjolfsson and McAfee conceptualize the "bounty" and the "spread" of technological innovation to describe the scope of the coming change. They underlie how the economy favors "superstars" and how even a marginal advantage in one market could lead to domination of the entire market in ways which were impossible before because of previous limitations of duplication and scale.[8]

Brynjolfsson and McAfee find that the economic downturn in 2008 only made for a perfect moment for firms to roll out labor saving technology because they had to fire workers anyhow. Could this be the reason for the 'jobless recovery?' They explain:

> Conversations with senior executives help explain this pattern in the data. A few years ago, we had a very candid discussion with one CEO, and he explained that he knew for over a decade that advances in information technology had rendered many routine information-processing jobs superfluous. At the same time, when profits and revenues are on the rise, it can be hard to eliminate jobs. When the recession came, business as usual obviously was not sustainable, which made it easier to implement a round of painful streamlining and layoffs. As the recession ended and profits and demand returned, the jobs doing routine work were not restored. Like so many other companies in recent years, his organization found it could use technology to scale up without these workers.[9]

They quote economist Wassily Leontief saying that "the role of humans as the most important factor of production is bound to diminish in the same way that the role of horses in agricultural production was first diminished and then eliminated by the introduction of tractors."[10]

Are these jobs being eliminated now not like most service jobs that take up so much of the 'post-Fordist' economy, service jobs like a secretary or a mid-level manager, parsimoniously shaved during the crisis by the economy's version of Occam's Razor?

Perhaps these were destined to disappear eventually anyhow. So many of the jobs which make up the 'post-Fordist' 'service economy' fit in nicely to what David Graeber has aptly described as 'bullshit jobs'[11] – the managers, office assistants, even lawyers to large businesses and so on which make up so much of the middle to upper strata of employment but without whom seemingly little of real economic value would be lost. Their persistence in such large numbers in a system that supposedly places the highest value on economic efficiency should be puzzling. Up until now their positions have been much less threatened than those of working class factory workers, teachers, and farmers, etc. who contribute much more tangible economic benefits. Until crisis culls the 'bullshit jobs' perhaps there is a level of human comfort in maintaining workers and positions that were held before. Perhaps the parsimonious Razor now has come for them too?

We all understand intuitively what happened in agriculture because of technology during the 20th Century. Work that used to take the efforts of many people was replaced by machines that could be operated perhaps by one person or even automatically. It was not just Leontiff's horse which was eliminated by the tractor. As a result, the vast amounts of labor which humans traditionally had dedicated to agriculture shifted. What once took 50% of the workforce in the United States, for example, now only takes around 2%.[12] Agriculture was just the low hanging fruit perhaps though in a much bigger story. While the labor which was once used for agriculture went into manufacturing as people moved into cities, now manufacturing labor is being done away with by the same forces of technology. As labor now shifts towards services, increasingly services too will be eliminated by advanced computer technology such as Watson; then where will labor go?

Perhaps people little appreciated the big picture here. The size of the coming shift and some of the latent frictions in how necessary employers view their workers have blinded people to what is really happening. Labor itself is becoming obsolete, a fossilized remnant of a previous age of civilization. The laborers though remain.

Workers are no longer strictly needed for work. As technology advances they will be needed even less. Still though, workers need work in our system of political economy.

In economic terms, technology will change the threshold at which economic value translates into new forms of work and benefits to society because capital has grown to substitute labor, which traditionally served as the conduit between economic growth and general well being. Capital will sever its most important link to social improvement if we do nothing to stop it.

What this means is that production which used to require human workers can now be done with a machine or a robot, considered a unit of capital owned by the capitalist, which requires no food, no healthcare, and takes no days off for vacation.

–

Water and Diamonds

To best understand the power of technology we should return to the previously mentioned Smithian 'water and diamonds paradox.' Technology can change the coordinates of what is scarce and what is valuable in the economy. If there were a hypothetical machine that indeed fulfilled what must have been a fantasy of some alchemist of yore and turned water into diamonds, the entire array of market prices of diamonds would be flipped on its head.

Imaginably diamond merchants probably would never want such a machine to ever exist. The marginal utility of diamonds would crash in the aftermath of such a machine. Labor occupies a similar position here to diamonds. The value of labor, once extraordinary, threatens to become merely ordinary once robots and highly productive machines change labor forever. If used in the wrong way, this could easily make technology a poisoned chalice.

There are many avenues towards which increases in productivity could go to of course. This is not necessarily a bad thing at all, in fact it is a wonderful thing that we have machines that are capable of doing work for us.

For example, machines could be used to reduce working hours in the day for everyone! If there is not enough demand for labor for everyone to work a full day, why not have everyone work half a day instead? This is what John Maynard Keynes anticipated productivity could go to.

The choice of industries about how they preferred to use their increased efficiency in production was clear though– to use technology to expand their enterprises, and to increase their global footprint and make money to the greatest extent that they could. They chose to boost profit, and the tradeoff was keeping labor hours as they were.

Is it any surprise that they chose this? It does not affect firms at all what workers' hours are or what unemployment looks like. Of course, considering what their position in society really is and how few their reciprocal legal obligations to that society really are, who could blame them for not caring? Doing what they have done with increased technological efficiency certainly resulted in the creation of the most marginal profit for companies and their stakeholders in the narrowly defined sense in which they operate – until the reckoning of economic crisis which they did not anticipate. That they, and not society, held the cards and made the decisions is the only issue to which we can object.

The question we face is the social question of what we do with technology – how do we cope with the inexorable changes which they have wrought on economic production, who controls production, and what incentives they face. The machines are here to stay. What we do with them is the only question.

–

The Luddite Dilemma

Technologies brilliant enough to create robots out of steel and genetically modified organisms which compete with what nature created are indeed powerful enough to change the course of human events. It is delusional to think that these new sorts of technologies signal nothing more than business as usual, or just any other stage of modernizing innovation. Innovation drives change, but the nature of that change and its impact on the economy depends significantly on the precise details of what is going on. Some innovations of the 20th Century complemented the skills and development of workers; these newest robotic technologies, however, certainly do not. This is not a wishful statement of values, but a sober statement of reality. New technologies substitute for human labor in ways which classical economics has too often denied were even possible. They conjure the spirit of the Luddite dilemma in ways which many economists are loath to ever admit.

Luddites were groups of craftsmen who went around destroying power looms in Northern England during the beginning of the Industrial Revolution. Protesting technology that would make their jobs obsolete, they have gone down as a symbol of irrational resistance to technology.

The Luddites were seen to have proven that all technological displacement is particular and not categorical, that it will not last forever, and that job losses caused by technology are limited to a few specific industries, which of course will quickly be replaced by others without causing a general loss of jobs in the economy. This assumption is generally accepted by economics. Because previous developments of labor saving technology did not reduce jobs in the long run, it must always be so. Even beyond particular trends in the job market, it is important to look ahead to foresee the consequences of automation.

Economics has simply not appreciated fully that there are specific differences between each stage of technological progress. These details of what exactly technology changes affect how technological innovation will impact jobs – time had just not yet come for categorical displacement of jobs, until now. The nature of these new machines is different and their changes to inputs in production much more extreme. The effects of new robots and computers in production are not necessarily analogous to 19th Century power looms.

Economics has made the mistake of assuming that because previous technological displacements were particular to only certain industries that it must always be like that. It has become assumed that it is impossible for technology to replace large, general swaths of jobs. As Martin Ford has shown though, the displacement of jobs by technology can indeed be total, just that this has not yet happened. This is an important distinction.

That the first steam engines and industrial mills had the effect of displacing particular jobs in hand loom industries is undeniable – an impact economics recognized while insisting these were just replaced by innovative factory jobs. Up until now, categorically displacing laborers was considered impossible following this logic. The Luddites' era was seen as proof of this – that all technological displacement is particular and not categorical, but in reality the threshold for categorical displacement had just not yet been reached. It may have a high bar, but not an insurmountable one.

This is a common mistake in economics – to conflate something with a high threshold with something that is impossible, or on the other hand something with a low threshold with something that is inevitable. See for example the unlimited demands assumption analyzed in the previous section.

Robots are the black swan of technological innovations. There is no previous comparison to the effects which robots will have on the economy and society, because they are categorically different than any previous form of technology. They represent not only a technological but a civilizational frontier. They are capable of producing without any continuous inputs from human labor. This is key. The difference between robots and earlier machines is that machines have often complimented human labor in at least some ways by requiring machine operators. Robots, however, by their very design do without them.

So with earlier machines even if the required amount of labor is reduced per unit of production with increased machine efficiency, so long as the amount of production rises by a high enough amount and in excess of the rise in population, as often has been the case under conditions of high growth, the demand for labor would keep up with the needs of the population. Thus, factory jobs replaced the jobs they destroyed (though the new jobs were different qualitatively).

Robots, by virtue of their automation, dispense of unneeded human input. They go further than older machines and completely replace the work of human laborers directly involved in the production of goods. This delivers huge swaths of human jobs to more efficient robots and leaves the old workers without work to do. Too many economists have denied that this can happen, but we only have to look at the evidence to see that this is already happening now and will speed up in the future.

The remaining machine operators and robot technicians who will still be required are too few in number to provide for a general source of labor even if everyone who is out of work trained to become a robotic technician or an engineer. The threshold of increased production required to employ everyone whose jobs have been lost to automation as new robot technicians would be unrealistically high, even if we assumed all of the old workers could be seamlessly retrained.

So those who insist that people who worked in manufacturing can just as easily receive education and training to do other jobs neglect to consider that since increased efficiency of technology is reducing the total number of workers needed throughout many sectors, while some new types of jobs will be created, they will be more than offset by the looming losses.[13] There will be a net loss of jobs.

Understanding these distinctions between the effects of robots and the effects of previous conventional machines seems to have eluded orthodox economic theory, and indeed most everyone else. The world requires a great paradigm shift that still has not been made, either by economics or by greater society, in order to adapt to a world of extraordinary new machines.

These robots are advancing into more and more fields of human economic activity, and not just the repetitive mechanical tasks which we associate with robots. As technology author Martin Ford has explained, robots will soon be appearing in fields as diverse as education, manufacturing, and medicine.[14] This is not the future projection of science fiction, but the sober assessment of economic leaders experienced in their fields. The beginning of these robots is the beginning of a new era. The Pandora's Box has been opened and we must find a way to live with and adapt to robots in the economy.

Ricardo's Insight

David Ricardo already had explored how machines are different from other categories of things in the economy two centuries ago. If we see Chapter XXXI of *Principles of Political Economy and Taxation*, he admits that while once he unquestioningly accepted the inevitable good of new labor saving machinery for everyone, "I am convinced that the substitution of machinery for human labour is often very injurious to the interest of the class of labourers."[15]

Much of what alarmed Ricardo during the first phase of the Industrial Revolution remains the same problem today. The issue as he describes it is that the economy is not like one giant organism, some Leviathan where the interests of all are combined so that which benefits one benefits all. This is, in fact, the entire problem. The economy is very much not like this.

Capitalism lacks a natural mechanism to make what is good for the Leviathan good for the individual. There is nothing to make what is good for the capitalist good for the worker. It is left to politics to make this happen.

So unsurprisingly it was a goal of the 20th Century's grand political projects to create this missing link – diverse ideologies take as their starting point that there is some blockage which prevents the economy from benefiting the people more generally. They just disagree about what this impediment is.[16] The imbalance in the economy unfortunately leaves much to the imagination, particularly as the capitalist ideology offers a circular 'just because' explanation for why markets ever generate bad outcomes. Social Democracy and Communism on the Left and Thatcherite Conservatism and Fascism on the Right all play with this idea, very tragically in the case of fascism, Nazism, and Stalinism.

As looked at in the previous section, the macro-economy operates as a whole, but individuals' finances are independent of each other. As Ricardo puts it, different parts of society operate with different accounts. What is good for the accounts of the capitalist might not be good for the accounts of workers. People's interests do not form an aggregate. Their individual interests do not correspond to what economists see as a social benefit to the whole from economic progress. In fact, because of how machines and advanced technology reorder the relationship between capital and labor, capitalists' and workers' interests will vary widely, and so there can be wide discrepancies in what benefits people get from technology, if any, under conditions of laissez-faire. Some people might even experience a loss. Of course, this is precisely what we have been seeing with technological development in some cases today.

Even if the net benefit is still positive from the introduction of new technology, as it inevitably should be, there could be wildly different effects on the holders of these different 'accounts' in society so "that the same cause which may increase the net revenue of the country may at the same time render the population redundant, and deteriorate the condition of the labourer."[17] It is not inconceivable that major technologies reorder market power and distribution so strongly in one direction that most people lose even as the economy on paper gains.[18] Technology which affects any industry which employs enough people could have this effect. As technology continues to advance, the consequences of these effects will only be magnified.

David Ricardo recognized the paradox that technological progress could actually be a net loss for many, or even most people in society if it adversely affects laborers.

His insight continues to prove true.

One thing that is for sure is that there is no going back to the comforting certainties, illusions perhaps, of the times before these technologies disrupted the rhythm of economic life, and of what work meant, forever. Technology has propelled the economy across the Rubicon. Society stands in awe before this transformation which has created a new era. If we have to drag this world kicking and screaming into the future, then so be it.

–

Work

For millennia the limiting factor in economic activity was work. The world was seen as a great boundless source of wealth, so that if only people put in enough work to extract resources from nature (or use them to fashion something useful) wealth would be theirs. Not anymore. Now the limiting factor in economic activity is demand. What changed?

Once technology made production and economic activity more efficient for cost, then work effectively became less scarce. Before there was always stuff to do that needed people to do it, but this is not necessarily always the case anymore. What we see in modern recessions and depressions is exactly that demand, the ability of society to want and be able to buy things which are produced, becomes the limiting factor on growth. As we have seen, demand is more contingent and subjective with things that people do not strictly need. Its absence causes unemployment when it falls below a certain level. The need for work recedes into the background as unemployment rises. Work, or labor, as an entire factor of production continues to become less scarce as technology progresses. The only countervailing force is an increase in goods demanded, which would have to be increasingly steep or labor intensive to overcome the increased efficiency of labor saving technology in production.

Growth is conventionally seen as the natural solution to technological unemployment. As we have seen in the previous section though, the expectation for the sort of never ending increase in demand for goods is not realistic. It will not sustain economic growth and certainly not previous levels of employment. Of course, this problem identified in the Great Depression by John Maynard Keynes and others is that this resulting lack of demand coupled with unemployment causes economic decline. This is effectively a modern difficulty which has come with industrialization. The technological situation we see today has undone a very ancient way of doing things and of conceptualizing work as a result.

Since the beginning of civilization work had always been the limiting factor in the economy. In essence work was the speed limit of the economy. Because of this, so long as people worked more, it was assumed that this would directly lead to economic growth. This is undoubtedly how the familiar imperative to work evolved which is more or less preserved in capitalism – the commonsensical idea that everyone should work hard to get ahead and contribute to society.

These days, with the current level of technological innovation, work is no longer relatively scarce. If we look at the economy as a set of different limiting factors of production, such as work, demand, resources, etc., we should see that technology has lessened the limitations arising from work while it has increased the restrictiveness of demand on growth. There are some mixed effects on resource constraints – some common resources can be extracted more easily while energy has become an important limiting factor of production. Now that the limiting factor on economic growth is generally demand, the economy has to adapt to a new world in which there may not always be work to do – despite our best attempts at pumping demand into the economy through quantitative easing and rock bottom interest rates. There really will be more workers than there is work as the future becomes the present. This is a revolutionary concept. If there is not always work to do, then there cannot always be enough to do for everyone who needs work either.

It might be said that there is work to be done but capitalism just is not properly assigning people to work. This is certainly true to some extent, and perhaps with public works projects, for example, more of the useful things that need to be done in society would get done – of which there are still plenty to do. Building infrastructure would be a good example. However, technology will impact the labor efficiency of these jobs as well. So unless people get paid to do something along the lines of digging ditches to fill them up again, technology will still inevitably impact jobs. So the fundamental problem remains.

What technology actually threatens most beyond any specific business or industry is an entire paradigm of looking at the world that has remained largely untouched since the Neolithic Era. Technology threatens to upend the very idea of work.

This is the idea that work generates progress and that by nature the more people work, the more production there will be, and the less people work, the less production there will be; if there is more production it must be the result of someone's hard work, and if people receive less it must be because they have not worked very hard.

Once work is no longer the limiting factor of production, this familiar paradigm ends because while someone can work very hard at a job, if there is enough downward pressure on the value of that work because of, say, automation, the market will not reward that work as much as it used to. Technology, particularly with automation, upends the idea stated by Rousseau in his *Second Discourse on Inequality* that work, or the need to work the land and produce new goods, is the trade off accepted in exchange for civilization and the price paid at the end of the state of nature.[19]

Technology destroys this entire very familiar way of

thinking about the world because with very advanced technologies such as robots *it is the robot which is doing work* and not any human. These robots lack agency, which only their human owners have, and in many cases the robots are not owned by any particular human, but by a large multi-national corporation, a legal construct, only indirectly owned by its investors.

The implications should give us a long moment of pause. Human workers are becoming less needed but not because there is less production going on, but because machines are filling the tasks of human labor. Machines of course are property of their owners. Not since slavery have capitalists *owned* their source of labor for production. The American Civil War's cause was partly the effect on free workers that labor *owned* by a landlord would have. The social implications are huge in this new environment for workers who rely on work for their livelihood. This is partly explored in the next section.

Humans have lived for thousands of years with the expectation that they would live the by sweat of their brow. Civilization emerged as a way to co-ordinate this, and many cultural mindsets one inscribed the social utility of work deeply into the social code, as Max Weber explored. Little wonder then it is that as our own Science has created new ways for work to be replaced and done for us, we have failed to adapt. We have found this awkward because it is highly counter-intuitive to adapt to a system where work is not central after it was so important for survival for so many centuries. To eliminate work we need a new phase in our great civilizations.

We have to accept the basic principle that robots will eliminate work. Not just certain workers, but a broad general amount of work will no longer be needed by society, even though this type of work has been necessary for thousands of years. The decline of agricultural labor in the 20th Century, once the bedrock of human work for millennia, presages the decline of manufacturing work and other work more generally. Farm workers declined from close to 50% of the working population in the United States to just a couple percentage points today as a result of automation. If that could happen in one area like agriculture there is nothing saying it cannot happen in other areas as well. Agriculture was first to adopt automation which reduced the number of workers it needed and moved people away from the land, and now other areas of industry are going the same way. Though agricultural work remains, and is often an unpopular and grueling job, its total share of the work done in society has collapsed.

The pursuit of co-operation needs to reach a new level at which work can be gradually abandoned by everyone in an acceptable way. Of course this will be a good thing. The same work that chains the human psyche to toil overproduces goods and often drives others out of their livelihood while it generates a glut of goods which causes the emissions that threaten to ensure that catastrophic global warming will come to pass.

For many people eliminating the imperative to work would still induce anxiety because work, at least for the many if not the most wealthy, has for so long seemed to be the foundation of civilized life.

It is our culture, our shared endeavor of human existence and of life together, and not work, which must always be at the indispensable centre of our societies though. *Creation*, distinguished from production, is what makes us human anyhow and now with technologies that change the place of production in society we are forced to confront this.

In many ways our problems lie precisely with the place we consider work to hold, and the ensuing confusion modernity imposes on us as it changes the role of work. Modernity intrudes into a settled world we thought we had been used to from the dawn of civilization.

Work overburdens our lives at any rate, a truth few would deny, and unnecessary work should not be missed. The imperative to work certainly also contributes to the planet's destruction because of the use of dirty industry and the needless extraction of resources. Instead of being considered a means to an end, work has appeared to be an end in itself for many. In so many ways if the world collectively stopped working so much we could solve many of our problems. The danger of death by overwork, what Japanese has called Karōshi, is very real for societies today.

New technologies like robots are clearly revealing why work has only ever been a means to an end, and not a 'reality of life' as it has often been seen, whether we are prepared to accept this or not. To use technology for the best possible purposes, and not the worst, is the challenge we face now. To best use technology we first have to acknowledge exactly its power. In order to rationally deal with our advanced level of technology the old assumption about work needs to be turned on its head.

–

Labor's Future

Labor is the main realm which will change in this world of robots and highly advanced technology. As work becomes forever changed by technology, the effect on labor will be inescapable. Economics recently has generally rejected a labor theory of value in a descriptive sense that explains why goods have value, but it has not addressed the prescriptive question of how labor *should be* valued by society.[20]

For ordinary people, work still has meaning. Society agrees. Economics has not given such a clear answer. The contradiction between the normative view of work and the objective economic value of work is striking. With new technology, people's work will mostly mean nothing. For the work that remains, much of it unpaid work that has fallen disproportionately on women and creative work that that gets precariously rewarded, capitalism has proven itself dismal at fairly distributing compensation. Reconciling our social vision of labor with the capabilities of technology will be a major challenge we grapple with as years go on.

Objectively speaking most people's wage labor could soon be done by a robot. There are exceptions. The exceptions, we see already, are entrepreneurial jobs and the jobs of certain highly trained 'experts' like the few technical experts needed to run the machines, and the certain lawyers, financiers, and business people who manage the system. Add to that of course many jobs that do not get paid. Everyone else, in an economic sense, becomes expendable.

This is the problem with technology in capitalism. Without labor theory of value, work fails to have any objective significance, something confirmed by current economic schools of thought and conditions we see in reality.

For politics and society, labor is still considered important. For capitalism under the current law though, people get in wages presumptively what the market considers the marginal benefit of their work, without any guarantee that this will end up amounting to anything. Technology will concentrate the powers of production into fewer and fewer hands, those of capitalism's owners and managers who hold ownership and control over productive machines, while leaving other people with nothing to offer, though society still considers it necessary for them to offer something which they can no longer offer in exchange for resources. To justify their existence in capitalism workers have to offer something. Technology leaves them in many cases with nothing to offer. With nothing to offer through their work many people will have nothing. We see this patent injustice already facing people all over the world in industrial towns where factories and employment have gone forever leaving behind their erstwhile workers as redundant orphans, the vestigial arm of the Leviathan that no longer finds a use for them. Theirs is a world of post-industrial night; the sun set on their world, their jobs, and by the logic of capitalism their whole communities. This is the future all of us face if we do not resolve the massive contradiction in the system we have today with how to properly apply technology for the greater benefit of humanity. Left to the capitalist Leviathan, we may all be made redundant to the Machine.

Technology can both create a wildly better, and more just world, or it can cause disruption, dislocation, and disaster for the vast majority of the world's people. Technology in the economy is about power. It is the power to produce more efficiently than we ever have done before, and also to create social upheaval. With great power comes great responsibility.

The Future for our Grandchildren

Here John Maynard Keynes provides a key insight. In the heyday of the Keynesian model and Social Democracy, economists predicted that with technological growth work would be gradually eliminated as machines began to improve life for everyone. Keynes' famous "Grandchildren Essay" foretold a fantastical world in which want and the whole economic problem would be eliminated by a new level of technological efficiency for producing human needs,[21] solving for what here has been called 'objective demand.' The world of tomorrow for Keynes would eliminate the need for hard labor and menial toil.

Machines are designed to produce what humans need more quickly, more cheaply, and more easily than doing things by hand, and so the logical result of increases in industrialization and machine use should be that the prices of human essentials fall over time. This should reduce demands on people's wages, while increased productive efficiency lessens the hours each day people need to work. At least this is the idea.

Of course this brings up the central paradox of technological efficiency. We see it borne out in the world today. Technology presents us a choice of what to do with efficiency. The Keynesian vision of the bright and verdant future relies on the same exact phenomenon which has been causing problems in advanced societies today and which was doing the same thing in the 1930's and the 1820's – technological unemployment.

The only difference between utopia and apocalypse, as happens so often, lies in how the windfall from revolutionary change is used by society – how technology is applied and distributed.

The choice today is whether to use technology to reduce work or to reduce workers. Stasis is not a choice. We can be misguided by our traditional view of work to apply technology for the wrong purposes, but it will possibly destroy us if we are not able to redirect it for the purposes it is really needed for.

The Keynesian vision of the future is the flip side of the coin of economic depression which we saw then and have seen now. This world of progress would be led by technology – as it should be. If only technology could be harnessed for what it really could do! This is how Keynes saw it and he described the Great Depression as a hiccup, a sort of unintended consequence, in the drive towards human progress.[22] Quite possibly, it is this same tendency from the advance in technology which contributed to the Great Depression which is driving the crisis in demand still.

As technology developed in the 1920's, there was a massive expansion in productive capacity which helped to fuel overcapacity. New types of industries, like the auto industry and the rise of new consumer appliances drove expansion.[23] They also drove speculation. Factories producing vast amounts of goods with new assembly lines could make these types of goods at a capacity that potentially exceeded the upper limits of consumer demand for them. Of course, these goods, by their virtue of making life easier for people, also increased the efficiency of life and presumably reduced demand for substitute goods which they were replacing. John Maynard Keynes hints that these factors may have contributed to the conditions at the beginning of the Depression, a glut in production and demand shortage that only became exacerbated once the market crashed and people lost their jobs and thus their source of income which fueled consumer demand for these products.[24] This is not an inevitable crisis created by technology though.

Solving this technological paradox requires that we allow technology to reduce the need to work for the benefit of everyone generally. We face a stark choice of doing this, or maintaining the current posture towards technology and letting its power coalesce at the top and destroy the fabric of society.

Keynes' prediction is so optimistic about the possibilities of technology he even speculates we might have problems finding things to do with all of our spare time, freed up from the chains of economic toil.[25] We can only begin to understand what might happen in this sort of society. Would all of our extra time be devoted to perfecting our interpersonal relationships with each other? Could a society of friendship centered on love for each other and humanity emerge from human liberation out of economic need? Or perhaps we could become builders – of things we actually love and not just of economic exigences.

Today many writers like Ray Kurzweil[26] have predicted a medical revolution in which we all could live for centuries with advances in medical technology and new forms of nutrition in advanced societies. Technologists have even speculated that we could download our consciousnesses onto a central computer, so that our minds live forever even when our bodies die.[27]

True immortality was only dreamt of by the ancient Egyptians as a spiritual power conferred by the gods. When the weight of a person's soul was measured on a scale against the weight of a feather by Anubis and Thoth, it was a spiritual power and the judgment of good and evil which determined fate. Technologists today believe in very material immortality for debatable but justifiable reasons. Human powers are approaching the realm of the gods. We are in some ways already god-like for someone seeing our world from the perspective of the Bronze Age.

We should like to think that in this sort of world we would become more loving, caring people with more time to pay attention to the true psychological and spiritual needs of each other. Perhaps with all of the pressing needs of humanity fulfilled, we could return to a more natural and harmonious existence in tune with nature and the passing cycles of time on Earth. There would really be a choice people could make regarding what to do with all of their new-found time – with the fewer restrictions on the amount of productive effort needed to create this world than the amount of resources used relative to the finite resources of the planet. All of this is not as absurd or far-fetched as it sounds. With the massive increases in productivity which have happened, we should be approaching this level of development, or at least be well on our way.

All the value created by our productivity should come to reward us. Many writers like Brynjolfsson and McAfee[28] have observed that the realization of this sort of world is coming closer to reality with the advent of recent technologies. The amount of goods produced could soon ensure freedom from want. The final step of our liberation, from economic need, is fully within our grasp, if we choose to take it.

If Keynes' world of tomorrow would eliminate the need for hard labor and menial toil, tomorrow is still another day. Any true humanitarian should be rightfully incensed about what has failed to happen and have a determination to find out what went wrong with what Keynesians had predicted would come into being by the year 2000. The technological-economic utopia predicted as a consequence of the mid-century advance in technology failed to materialize.

Technology is certainly on track, at least for the most part. There may not yet be flying cars (though there really could be, in a technical sense). The internet would have been unfathomable though for someone writing in the 1930's. So while the pace of technology has varied in different areas, the overall the trend of advancement has occurred.[29] It cannot be said that technology has underperformed Keynes' expectations.

The economy has failed. How so? Our progress in material production has been misappropriated. Instead of being used to make life easier (which technological progress has always sworn to be its aim), as even the first wave of the Industrial Revolution in the British clothing industry promised to do, the increases in efficiency have been diverted. They have gone into increasing the scale of economic production for corporations, with the aim of selling more stuff to more people for more profit for fewer people.[30] The economy has been directed towards making more stuff over making life easier. The type of stuff made is not the stuff that we most need to free ourselves from want, but the sort which corporations most need for increased private growth.

We see this mostly clearly shown in productivity numbers.[31] Productivity has risen consistently all while wages have stayed constant. The predictions by the mid-century economists that technology would reduce the amount of hours worked in the day have largely not come to pass. While in some places experiments in shorter working hours have taken place, for example at some workplaces in Sweden where this has been implemented,[32] the long eight hour day is still generally the norm, particularly outside Europe. Meanwhile, for corporations, profits reveal that they indeed are using the tools of increased efficiency for their benefit.

The Robot's Dawn

Eminent British physicist Stephen Hawking has stated that the real threat from technology is not of a robot takeover, like in the theory of the 'singularity,' but of the misappropriation of robots which destroys the humanity of most of the human race by giving unbelievable power to the top percentage of people who own the machines and the robots.[33] Whoever owns the machines owns humanity.

The earliest work of literature to refer to the word robot deals with exactly this situation. The word robot derives from a 1920's Czech play by Karel Čapek called *Rossum's Universal Robots*. The new word robot derives from a word that translates into English as serf, or servant.[34]

As featured in this play, the company Rossum's Universal Robots specializes in the manufacture of robots. It spreads robots around the world for sale and drastically alters how the world economy functions. The new robots quickly replace all of the mechanical tasks done by humans. Weirdly similar to what technology does today, these robots produce on their own and render working people obsolete, though the replacement of human labor is much more absolute than what we see in the present situation so far. Humans are left with little to do at all.

All of the traditional labor of humans becomes appropriated by robots and the robot class. The old role of humans merges into the new role of the robots. While humans' role is usurped by the technology of their science's own creation, confusion reigns over a world where the line between human and robot fades. Society does not know how to deal with this.

The robots emerge out of synthetic life molds, yet appear exactly like humans and not like a computer or a mechanical android.[35] Like computers of today these robots envisioned in Čapek's 1920's play can do instantaneous computations that would take humans much longer. Any mechanical task is done better and faster by a robot. Robots work; they appear like humans, but they are not human. By virtue of being a robot they lack the most important characteristics of living humans which are exclusively human – will, desire, ethical thought, and love. As the productive powers of the robot increase, it is exactly these powers exclusive to the human mind which acquire newfound importance.

Old Rossum created the robot for science. He dreamt of a world where new beings removed the theological underpinnings of God from creation. His son knew that robots would make money though, too much money to keep them as a sophisticated science experiment.

Many of the themes that are still debated today in philosophy of mind appear already in Čapek's play. Could a robot constructed exactly of the same parts as a human being possibly become a human, or would there be something still missing? Would sentience be innate or need to be designed, if it is even possible to do so? The ethical dilemmas of robots outlined by Isaac Asimov appear in *Rossum's Universal Robots* when the robots take up arms.[36] The danger of these robots, like those of Artificial Intelligence generally, is of a goal oriented machine programmed for potentially destructive ends without the broader reasoning powers of humans.

Of course, these are also the fears from the time of Mary Shelley's *Frankenstein*, of the emergence of a creature neither living nor dead, brought into the world through science but not fully understood by it. These are fears of a modern technological monster, and robots fill the role of this Frankenstein monster quite well. Could this monster created by humanity come back to haunt humanity? What the ethical and ontological dilemmas of such a creation are seem to feature front and center for Karel Čapek. Most worrying is what humans would do with the robots though – and how this could spiral out of our control. Tales like these are never just about a creature. How could one person who makes a private decision over powerful robots with centralized decision making power and the capacity for creating collateral consequences possibly affect the fate of the entire planet?

The distinctive word robot was allegedly coined by Čapek's brother, as a more authentic sounding word than the Latinaic alternative word *automat*. If a robot is a servant, then the real ethical question is whose robot it is. If a robot is a servant, then who is the master?

The double meaning as a technological robot, and as a bonded servant is very revealing, perhaps more so than Karel Čapek or his brother would have realized.[37]

The robot completely upends assumptions made by classical liberal economics as we see by eliminating the need for human workers to act as labor, and in fact entirely eliminating labor as an indispensable factor of production. This is the robot's real power. The robots become the willing servants of whoever their master may be. If the masters of the machines shall be us all, or only a select few stands as the real question and the monumental dilemma.

Labor, wages, and work are all replaceable in the long run. It is no longer a matter of if but when technology will chip them away. The implications of course could be devastating. As Martin Ford pointed out, assuming the laws of capitalism remain as they are now, without the need for the part of the economic system known as labor technology will hollow out the entire economic ecosystem because there would not be any mechanism for money to flow between different parts of society anymore, mainly because of so many who are dispossessed non-owners of vital machines.

Without the need for human labor there would be no need for wages or for any money to flow from the top to any other part of society which is not an owner of resources. A couple of trends follow, both of which we already see. First, this would concentrate more of the wealth of society at the very top rung of owners and managers who control the machines and vital resources. Secondly though, it could paradoxically collapse demand because there would not be a group of consumers able to buy the products of machines without a 'middle class' of people who receive wages from labor.[38] With the limiting factor of economic progress as demand in this world, there is a possibility that the current trajectory could collapse the entire economy without some mechanism ensuring that more efficient ways of production benefit more than just a narrow slice of owners who have little use for the rest of society. Of course the greatest use owners, investors, and managers of machines do have for the rest of us is as customers, so even they really do have a reason to support avoiding this worst possible outcome too, lest the Crisis of Demand expand to consume them as well.

Technological benefits may increase overall productivity, but *for whom*? This question *for whom* technology benefits and for what purpose is not an empty question. It is, on the contrary, the most important question in the economy today. Technology creates a massive social disruption, and so technological advances require a complete retheorization of the economic social contract. A democratic debate about how technology is used is conspicuously missing.

Economic Purpose

Keynes foresaw this, as did Marx. It is this level of disruption by modernity, particularly if exacerbated by an economic recession, that Marx predicted would lead to a proletarian revolution.[39] While in Marx's time the working class proletariat stood as the necessary input in production without which the system could not function, now such a Marxian revolution would be staged by what could be called only the ex-proletariat, laid off factory workers who no longer comprise a key strategic position. As such it would have much less chance of success unless done in a country with an exceptionally concentrated industrial workforce like China. While Marx in many ways underestimated the true scope of technology to come, Keynes, as previously stated, saw the advance of technology but largely did not see the direction in which it would flow. Keynes' techno-optimistic prediction is an unfulfilled promise.

As developed countries' factories become more automated, the profile of labor needed is different than it used to be. Truly low wage industrial work has moved to Asia, but even without that happening, there would have been a collapse in the industrial labor base as a result of technology. Factories require fewer workers and instead need technicians who can run and fix the machines and highly educated specialists who can design them or manage the economic proceeds of their output. However, this is far from an even trade off. The new profile of jobs is much slimmer than the old one was. And without occupying the privileged proletarian position in political economy that it used to, labor has little power to stage a strike to maintain redundant jobs that technology has disposed of. At the very least it is losing its relative bargaining power in rich countries.

This has slowly created the unenviable situation in which many developed countries have more people requiring well paying jobs than there are appropriate jobs to give them. Eventually, this will happen in developing countries as well. The advance of 'service sector' jobs has not nearly kept pace with the loss of old style manufacturing jobs, and this has deep political implications in the West that cannot be ignored, with the advance of political forces such as Trump and Le Pen.

In the Social Democratic system and the 19th Century industrial capitalist system, there was a semblance of balance of labor jobs to people. Typically, the head of a household could work at a job which carried enough bargaining power to provide for a traditionally sized family.

Automation takes away this economic certainty. A sense of disorientation results from a shift in economic organization. People seek a degree of certainty in their lives, on a socio-economic level and otherwise. Many of the interpretations of the new technological economy have predicted that people will just adapt to constantly looking for new work as robots or other new technology renders them obsolete. This is not always the case though. Without a share of the proceeds of the new technological property regime, people will inevitably become dislocated and discontented as their whole world collapses without a replacement forthcoming. This might not need be such a problem with the advent of technologies that have the promise to vastly make life easier, except for the fact that technology's benefits are being completely steered by the very rich property owners who control the new technology for their own benefit, and not the general benefit of society.

In more of a social than economic sense, the need to understand the rules, to belong, and to believe in something is strong. Economic change that disrupts a society's communal life, traditional industry, and even sense of virtue can cause severe social problems. It is about more than just efficiency.

We can see for example with Greenland's industrialization in the middle of the last century, the move from the village to Nuuk and from being a hunter to working in an office disrupted people's sense of identity, and resulted in an explosion of suicides.[40] This happened even though the development of Greenland brought it supposedly in line with the standards of Denmark and other rich countries.

The same drastic harms which came with industrialization also come with the current trends of de-industrialization in the developed world. In many ways the United States and the Soviet Union were the two paradigms of the 20th Century 'Fordist' modern economy built on massive scale and industrial-technological know-how. We know about the social problems created by the Soviet collapse in 1991. Is the pattern of de-industrialization in the United States not similar? As factories and jobs leave the Midwest whole towns are eviscerated which has caused a crisis in drugs, health and education, and even masculinity as the mainly working class and middle class men who were socialized to think of having an industrial job providing for a traditional family are left confused and without a purpose.[41]

We should fear the potential political backlash from this. Is this economic shift not partly responsible for the surge in nationalism across countries where overt nationalist politicians were non-existent just a decade ago? The rise of nationalist parties to power in Poland, Hungary, and even India should warn us of what could happen elsewhere. Is Donald Trump not the response to people's yearning for order, even if it is a sort of authoritarian order? Is it not a demand for a country where they have a place again? In Russia is Vladimir Putin not making the same offer to the same groups of people left behind in the same way nearly 30 years ago?

With Donald Trump's election as President of the United States, the advance of Marine Le Pen to the Second Round of the French Presidential Election, and the rise of numerous varieties of nationalist governments around the world calling to 'bring the jobs back' we should see the real political consequence of doing nothing in the face of the social catastrophe of de-industrialization. The people who remain left behind by the last industrial capitalist order will not sit quietly while they suffer. For venal political forces keen to take advantage of their anger and hopelessness for nefarious purposes, they are an easy target.

Those left behind could be a natural constituency for a hopeful and egalitarian democratic uprising as well, if one were to seriously speak to them. In the United States, Bernie Sanders' Presidential campaign showed how a movement of hope that seriously pushes for broad reforms that promote equality and benefit the working class could win. He won across the deep American political, social, and racial divides, and there is a very good chance that if his movement had continued into the General Election he would have given hope to the hopeless who were convinced they had no better choice than to vote for Donald Trump.

–

The Crossroads

This leaves us at a crossroads. Either we use technology to relieve the burden of human work, or technology will destroy human livelihood by enriching the top echelon of society that owns it at everyone else's expense.

In Fritz Lang's *Metropolis*, there exists a society divided by technology and a yawning gap between the owner managers of society and the workers who literally toil down below.[42] The social compact lies in tension on the theatre of machines and modern technology, until it finally breaks... a final demand for transcendence, the "mediator between the head and the hands must be the heart."

What mediator though? To eliminate the paradox of machines in society, there needs to be an emergence of something new to rise out of the ashes of the old order machines replace, a unity in love of all interests.

The same tension between the true purpose of technology and an elite's fatally flawed calculus for using it defines the problem with machines and technology today. While *Metropolis* shows workers resembling a Marxian proletariat necessary for the functioning of the Machine in more ways than one, today's workers exist more along the lines of a 'precariat' of people without a place and extraneous to the machine. With the number of full time workers needed to sustain economic output low and probably going much lower, there has to be a redrafting of the social contract.

What we need more than anything is an ethical transformation in society that acknowledges the fact that technology should exclusively be used to *make life easier*. Our current system resists letting technology make life easier, because it tends to concentrate the benefits of technology too strongly – into the hands of those with very different incentives. Ownership of machines is not democratic. The requirement to work ensures that people will suffer from the effects of labor saving technology instead of enjoying its benefits. Reasonable alternatives to the requirement to work which acknowledge the inevitable economic position of labor saving technology have yet to be fully explored. So long as the concentration of capital ensures that the benefits of technology are locked up with the very richest in society, the owners of the technologies, the possibility of its effects going towards the society as a whole remains distant.

Until there is a way to ensure that the products of technology are jointly owned or shared, the effect of technology on society will inevitably be chaos and, eventually, conflict. As technology is used by the most powerful to consolidate their dominion over the rest of society, and indeed the world, there will be unending conflict. As perhaps we have seen as well with globalization, the losers of this system will not accept their fate or blindly go away, and the winners will not give up their privileges without a fight.

This is the role which politics must fill. The distribution of new technologies is inevitably a political question which society will have to answer. It can only do this very directly, through discourse about the role of technology, not just through a referral to the 'magic of the market' to sort out the problem, otherwise the owners will inevitably just appropriate technology to themselves for their own narrow benefit.

We have to understand that the world is different than it used to be, and reform the ways in which technology is misused. It can be used for ill as well as good. Technology is always just a tool – often a double edged sword. Technology is a means to an end.

Part III – The Reformation

One October day 500 years ago, in Saxony, a young German cleric struck a nail into the church door of Wittenberg's *Schlosskirche* and forever changed a world in which fundamental change seemed impossible. In Wittenberg, this young cleric named Martin Luther emerged from a maelstrom of philosophical debate over the true nature of a 'universal Church' – a Church whose institutions seemed thoroughly corrupted in purpose, which operated in a reality of indulgences and graft, and which had strayed so far from its original purpose so as to be unrecognizable to many of its adherents.

The Reformation had begun. When Martin Luther posted his 95 theses to the door, the Medieval Church was torn asunder. Luther's Reformation swept away the whole paradigm of more than a thousand years. The collapse of the Church of the Middle Ages altered the course of European civilization.

System change on a level like this inevitably occurs through institutions. As Reformers took control of the Church and rewrote the Christian theology, or in their minds perhaps restored it, a new sort of Church emerged. There was an ideological shift. Out of this came a great change – The Reformation. Like in other singular events of massive change like the French Revolution and the Russian Revolution, changes in the institutions afterwards created – or failed to create – what was really revolutionary.

Luther and Lutheranism sparked fundamental changes in the way society was structured. The collapse of the authority of the Church in Rome to collect tithes and indulgences in Northern Europe along with the forfeiture of Church property to secular control were the most obvious examples. The real change once again though was ideological. Out of the detritus of Medieval Christianity in Protestant countries came a different of the world. The 'priesthood of all believers' shifted the presumed control over the fate of the soul from the Church institution and tradition to the individual. The social changes from this shift in mentality were massive.

The effects would also alter the Catholic Church as it adapted to an evolving new theology. Early Church reformers, Jesuits, and later groups like Jansenists continued to shape the Catholic theology in response to The Reformation so that the institutions of the Middle Ages were changed fundamentally.

Not that this came out of nowhere. There was a deep crisis of spiritual authority at the end of the Middle Ages. This crisis had been developing over centuries. The Avignon Papacy, gradual corruption, and previous 'heresies' had hollowed out the claim of the Church in Rome to be the universal wellspring of truth and reason in Northern Europe. Luther had been influenced by a line of other reformers like Andreas Bodenstein von Karlstadt and intellectuals like Erasmus. For 100 years there had existed a living experiment of Church reform among the Hussites in Bohemia just to the South of Luther's home in Electoral Saxony. Some Taborites had attempted radical democratic and even some communistic Church reforms a century before that went far beyond what Luther was advocating.[1]

Yet Luther lit a spark that ignited the greatest Medieval institution and quickly overtook Germany and much of the rest of Europe. Reformation is possible. After a fermentation of many centuries fundamental change can happen quickly.

On a very different October day 100 years ago, another change swept away a great social order, even more swiftly. The Bolshevik Revolution took power in St. Petersburg and eventually in all of Russia. Though it quickly failed in its lofty aims, for a brief moment there was "all power to the Soviets." Though Lenin succeeded politically his vision quickly collapsed in political chaos after his death with maladaptation to material and social conditions and Stalin's despotism. Lenin's aims were unfulfilled. Tragedy ensued.

Nonetheless the February and October Revolutions changed world history forever. The fall of the Tsars ended centuries of autocrats and then the collapse of the Provisional Government moved Russian history in a very different direction from the Republic it might have created had the Bolsheviks never come to power.

The Russian Revolution proves how foolish it is to doubt that change is always possible – that an order which seems unchangeable could last forever. It shows how foolish it is to assume that an order which seems so improbable could never be. It shows that failure out of the jaws of triumph is always possible. Of course it also cautions us to the problems of easy answers to deeply structural problems. The Winter Palace might have been taken in one night of Revolution, but it is only the morning after when the first challenges of a new society present themselves. No great transformation in the economy can really happen overnight, and in Russia the promise of a democratic economic reformation both effective and egalitarian has still been left unfulfilled.[2]

We face a similar situation in the 21st Century to these moments preceding great social change. To successfully reform our economic institutions and create a new world, it is our mission in the 21st Century and our somber duty to create change, manage it successfully, and avoid mistakes people have made before. No conservative rearguard action will be able to resist change either with everything that is happening in the world today – and any sustained effort to change nothing will fare no better than the Tsar did when trying to stop the Duma from forming in a time of profoundly changing conditions. The world confronts the dual crisis of an economic transformation and an ecological disaster in capitalism – along with the moribund ideology which led us to this moment. The reality is that this will create great change for the world, and it will happen whether people like it or not. The question is just how we handle it. Like the events of both 100 and 500 years ago, we face an inflection point in world history in the making for many years and we are confronted with changing the social order. To create a new system to save our climate in particular, great change will be inescapable. Ecological sustainability with economic justice and utility demands a system change of the kind which we have undertaken at great moments in history and there is no use denying it is possible or necessary. History here can be our guide.

The two monumental world events of 100 and 500 years ago though seemingly distant might not be considered so different from each other. The necessity for great change to a system unresponsive to new needs and conditions was their common thread. This connection did not go unnoticed either. Before the Russian Revolution, in 1897 Karl Kautsky wrote *Communism in Central Europe in the Time of the Reformation* about the economic and social basis of the Protestant Reformation, particularly the radical egalitarian projects of groups among the Taborites and Anabaptists. He considered The Reformation in light of his contemporary socialist movements he and saw in both a common heritage of struggle against corrupted elites to make a just and rational society.[3] This perspective did not start history with industrialization.

The Reformation dealt at times in a radical way with the inequity of society and social hierarchy that was no longer necessary and could just as easily be dispensed with. Thomas Münzer's theology inspired a revolutionary German Peasant's

Revolt. Luther may have failed to support it and detested it but he nonetheless inspired it. Hussites sought to expropriate the lands of the Church that seemingly benefited only those in the Catholic hierarchy far away in Rome, occasionally in an egalitarian fashion but often not, much like later established Protestant Churches like the Church of England. Though often these truly radical reformers were just factions and were overtaken by the interests of the powerful, at stake for everyone was the question of the basic make up of society. Asking this question was itself half of The Reformation.

Change is inevitable. Under changing conditions, particularly when there a disconnect exists between material and social realities, without reform a social order will collapse under its own weight in a revolutionary explosion. This has happened before and it will happen again.

The global economy of the 21st Century is mired in its own corruption of purpose. Capitalist markets' rules of the game are outdated and do not reflect the current technological and social realities. The current matrix of interconnecting market incentives fails to direct corporations to produce in socially optimal ways. The system most benefits a corrupted upper echelon. The conditions which rise out of scientific and technical advances threaten our future world with all they entail – of environmental destruction and poverty from economic displacement. This requires a fundamental reformation of the incentives which guide economic development.

Conditions change. As they change the world around it must evolve as well to sweep away old ways of thinking that no longer function for their intended purpose. Reform is necessary now. The aims of this Economic Reformation should be clear.

For lack of a better way of understanding it, we need a system of material relations that gives people what they really need but currently lack. The materialism underlying our current economy fails to do this. People's unbalanced relation to material in rich countries swings between an extreme of oversaturation with material to a persistent lack of fundamental needs, or both at the same time. The bias shown by corporate incentives towards one kind of self-serving materialism ultimately negates the materialism of fulfilling basic needs well by an efficient use of resources.

The corporation, jobs, the ideology of growth – these are all ultimately flawed *mediators* between the people and their access to resources. Society sanctioned these mediators to send resources to the right places but inevitably they have come to distort needs around their own venal interests.[4] In reality powerful people and corporations created haves and have-nots whose fate need not correspond to their efforts, talents, or virtues – and their concentration of capital and increasingly their command of technology allows them to do this and warp the societies which supposedly benefit from them. Through their privileged position directing the economy from the top, they are viewed as intrinsically efficient at creating, rewarding, and distributing economic benefits – but if they really cannot do this, perhaps we should endeavor to cut them out, and restore a direct personal link between the individual and their real material needs. The more direct access people have to control over the machinery of capital the less their access to resources will be distorted by the build up of capital since industrialization. Democracy will then finally be extended to work.

Structured around the needs of the people first and foremost, the economy should endeavor to deliver material needs free of intermediaries, while freeing up space in people's lives for non-materialistic pursuits which they can fill their time with. A more optimum distribution of resources allows economics to fulfill people's basic objective needs while imbuing life with the intangible qualities of affection, love, togetherness, and creativity that make people truly happy.

To be sure, this implies a shift of consciousness around materialism. A materialism that focusses on what material is most useful for humanity at increasingly high levels of productive efficiency would cause itself to eventually fade into the background of human life. This materialism would do more than pile up more and more goods disconnected from real need. Thereby society can transcend materialism. We can no longer merely survive but live. The ultimate goal is to create an economy in which materialism gradually abolishes itself.

As the economy unlocks the material shackles around humans, we also resolve the fundamental paradox of rights under liberalism since the French Revolution. What rights do you really have if inequality deprives you of resources and leaves no choice but to work for corporations created by capital that command massively unequal bargaining power? The fewer material needs left unfulfilled the more liberty really flourishes.[5]

The time constraint for acting is becoming constrained of course by the tightening noose of devastating climate change.

Perverse Incentive & Market Power

Creating the sort of system change we need requires having a clear head about the economic big picture. We have to think holistically and systematically to understand some essential aspects of economic decision making which others choose to look away from. First we should recapitulate what incentives companies face.

It should be clear why companies want to use technology to produce more stuff. They only make money when transactions occur. Companies make money off of buy and sell events. This is what Karl Marx once described as the MCM exchange process of money-commodities-money which generates profit.[6] Without this, there is no possibility to make money. Firms need to sell something to make money or otherwise offer something which others will pay money for (through rent, etc.) To make money through commerce firms need to have something to offer. Barring a strong enough point of diminishing returns and the limits of demand, this incentive to produce extends indefinitely. This creates a problem. There exists here a wide gap between where companies' interests lie in generating transaction events and where the interests of the people and the planet lie with regards to what the products of industry should go towards.

Material production is the main point where the contradictory incentives between the largest firms and the people are apparent. This affects the economy as well as the climate of course. It shows a sharp break of interests between companies which want to use material to maximize their own present profit and people who have very specific and real material needs which objectively need to be fulfilled before other goals can be satisfied. Only 'natural' persons will feel the future 'externality' effects of economic crisis and climate change.

Technology's most socially useful applications often do not make money. Others create valuable monopolies. We see this play out with energy efficiency and with pharmaceuticals. Capitalism will direct focus to uses which can be enclosed for profit and overlook those which cannot. The imperative to produce more goods for profit has thereby often excluded the alternative possibility of easier production and extra free time in people's lives, despite the added benefits to social utility that this would create with the use of less energy.

Faced with the opportunities of new technologies, the problem is that the response of the market and corporations to new production possibilities has been completely irrational, at least from the standpoint of the general interest of the people. It is hopelessly ridden with perverse incentive. The profit motive often actively encourages companies to do things that are bad for human societies, not do good things which would come at the opportunity cost of not yielding enough enclosable private profit. It drives corporations to undercut the costs of others in ways that will only cause harm to wages and the environment as an externality to money making production. To the extent that it does this it cannot be considered a truly efficient allocator of resources, as it so often claims to be.

It should be asked why socially beneficial uses of technology are not promoted by competing companies. We see some examples of course. Tesla as previously mentioned creates cars with the goal of mitigating climate change firmly in the minds of its customers and this affects the rest of the market. Still though it holds very little market share and the pressure to shift away from internal combustion engines is being pushed harder by civil society pressure and certain governments concerned about climate and pollution, such as

India and France agreed to in a recent initiative, and not market forces which are mostly only reacting to the pressure.[7]

Of course this is explainable because with increased productive efficiency companies face a choice. By increasing the scale of production, they can offer more things to sell and increase their profits. Reducing working times on the other hand, for example, though in the interest of workers, has no effect on them at all and comes at an opportunity cost.[8]

The firms – even if they were inclined to keep production levels the same and divert extra savings from efficiency into shorter working times out of traditionalism or concern for workers – are effectively placed in a prisoner's dilemma if left to make the decision alone. They are strongly incentivized by the incentives all competing companies face to increase production with each technological advance, particularly if they are large and could face declining market share if they do not follow suit. Some companies with a niche market for doing business in old or traditional ways will resist, usually marketing themselves for premium customers, but most cannot. The result is a walk down the garden path that careens into a race to the bottom of how to best use more efficient technology to make more stuff for more profit.[9]

The interest of the people is not represented in this decision. Power over production decision making lies with those who own production and their choices are self-evident.

Increases in leisure time are not enclosable. Workers' freetime is an inalienable part of themselves. Time off is not enclosable for a firm and, thus, made into a profitable commodity. So the more time people have free is a straight loss for corporations which *could be* used to make new profitable commodities instead. An increase in leisure time thus represents an opportunity cost for the corporation.[10]

Since making life easier for workers is a dead end for most firms, companies have focused on transforming new productive efficiencies into economies of scale and scope to sell more products, with wide ranging consequences. Because of the incentives large firms face and because of their immense power over decisions of how resources are used, we see how the ecological crisis which should be the first priority of the economy to solve is placed on a secondary tier of importance and that we are needlessly overworked far beyond what is required for social utility.

We see here the driving reason behind the failure of the Keynesian promise in "The Future for our Grandchildren." The incentive structure companies face to produce and the concentration of market power with them put important decisions about the large scale direction of the economy in the hands of those who have no interest in "The Future for our Grandchildren."

So while for workers, having a four hour day while achieving the same level of productivity reached under old industry in eight hours would be fantastic and is very much in their interests, it is totally opposed to the interests of capitalist firms. Barring some special circumstances, the result is that corporations will resist turning more efficient production technologies into shorter working hours so long as they decide. The different bargaining power between workers and corporations ensures that the interests of the corporations will prevail. While this entire situation arising from technology seems counter-intuitive, Jean Jacques Rousseau largely foresaw exactly this pattern emerging out of the advancement of technology even in the 18th Century – how the incentives towards acquisitiveness could effectively misdirect advances in technology towards unforeseen ends to concentrate power.

Is this result just what the people really want? No.[11]
People want more leisure time and, objectively, voraciousness
for stuff should be reaching its logical upper limit. The drive
for capitalist firms to make more stuff is becoming dangerous
and is of course against the people's interest because this is
what also drives the growth of carbon emissions and climate
change. Our consumption of material goods is hitting the
ecological limits of the planet's ability to sustain it. This is
sadly fueled by technology which has allowed us to make
more stuff more quickly and cheaply than ever before, though
it could be used instead to fulfill our old level of needs more
easily, cheaply, and consistently than before while setting us
free from the levels of work previously needed to achieve this.

We live in a society where the people do not get to
choose what it uses technological powers for. These are too
often the decisions of corporations over which people have no
power. It always suited corporations who produced stuff to
make even more stuff with higher efficiencies so they can sell
it. So this is what they have done and continue to do to the
detriment of the people and the wider economic interest. The
impacts include inequality, economic crisis, and destruction of
the climate. It is this perverse incentive which the law must
evolve to combat. The universal pursuit of humanity is
freedom but our economic system forms the antithesis of this
freedom, and in this derogation of humanity lies the
contradiction at the heart of our supposedly democratic
societies. To solve for this is the end of economic reformation.

The Law

The obvious question now is how society would affect such an economic reformation. There are some obvious historical examples of massive changes to the economy which have come about as a result of a movement for economic reform. The Keynesian Welfare State provides a good example, as do co-operatives like Mondragon in Spain which have operated since the early 20th Century. The reformation needed now cannot simply be a copy of these previous economic models though. Both of these are insufficient to the task of governing and managing the scale and scope of the problems the world's economy faces today. Neither provides quite what needs to be changed to fix it, though no political revolution is necessary to create a solution either.

The emergent conditions of the modern economy which have led up to the crisis act on a theatre which could be called *the law*. Legal rights and obligations shape economic incentives and create this system of incentives we understand as capitalism. The law played a critical role in the emergence of modern capitalism. It frames what is and is not sanctioned by society. Law is not the same thing as the political system, though they are closely related, but it is the structure that guides and sanctions social relations and it evolves over time as new conditions demand it to. This is the locus where the conceptually simplest and yet also most far reaching reformation regarding the economy could be made. The law is a crucible that creates the structures of economic relations, between buyers and sellers, workers and employers, the people and the Earth we live on. Its underlying doctrines evolve throughout history.

Society sanctions economic activity and policy through the law. Social expectations set in law can affect basic economic behavior, even in seemingly neutral and dispassionate areas. Brazil's hyperinflation of the 80's and 90's[12] shows an excellent example of this, with the society's official posting of 'real' prices changing the psychological expectation of ever increasing price rises – an interesting example of convergence between the 'reality function' and the 'manipulative function' of markets.

Law structures the 'rules of the game' of capitalism and by changing certain fundamental laws the structure of the economy can be effectively reformed without a political revolution needing to happen.

Very basic and fundamental changes in the law can happen and have happened through a process of reformation, such as the elimination of slavery, enslavement of human beings gradually becoming accepted internationally as a violation of an important *jus cogens* norm in the 19th Century. This overrode vile and indefensible claims that people could be held as property. The triumph of a higher pre-emptory moral law adopted throughout the world effectively eliminated slavery from the economy.

Institutions of capitalism, though touted as 'natural' by their supporters, are nothing more than a legal construct which evolve and can be fundamentally reformed through social progress and political action.

–

Capitalism as a Historical System

A quick overview is necessary of what capitalist institutions are and how they came to be. Capitalism is not one single entity, but the result of an evolution of laws. It was not created in one moment, but over an era through the development of different parts of the legal system which sanctions through the law what we would call 'Capitalism'. While Marxist scholars for example have argued that the French Revolution was a 'bourgeois' revolution, a particular event which enshrined the interests of the bourgeoisie as the interests of the modern state in the form of capitalism, the underlying conditions which crated the possibility for this 'bourgeois revolution' stretched back for centuries before that.

The Dutch Republic in the 1600's developed some of the first examples of what we might call capitalist markets. The Dutch Republic featured the first insurance exchanges, for life insurance on maritime voyages. The Dutch also traded shares on the Amsterdam Stock Exchange, the first modern stock exchange, and they traded shares in the Dutch East India Company among others which was one of the first real corporations. This corporation differed from similar institutions like what the Early Modern banking families such as the Medicis or the Fuggers had because, first, the Dutch East India Company was not just a family business engaged in banking but a public company, and, second, it issued shares. It even represented itself with what we could consider an easily identifiable company logo – an interlocking VOC. This company, the *Vereenigde Oost-Indische Compagnie*, was effectively the world's first multi-national corporation after which subsequent corporations were modelled.

The Medici family functioned more like a banking cartel by contrast which assumed control of state power in the

City of Florence; the Dutch East India Company maintained a separate though largely incestuous legal relationship with the Dutch State and the City of Amsterdam (along with other port cities). Its owners were ultimately its shareholders. People would buy stock in the company and then the company returned dividends as a benefit to its shareholders. Later British and Americans would expand on some of these key innovations from early joint stock companies like the VOC, particularly developing industrial capitalism as a refined system of legal structures that built on the innovations the Dutch maritime trading republic had created for maritime trade.[13]

In France as well, the power of the bourgeoisie had grown significantly for what we could call structural reasons over the 18th Century. Significant bourgeois figures like Madame de Pompadour, Louis XV's glamourous and powerful mistress, reached the highest levels of government and power even in 'aristocratic' France of the Bourbon monarchy as money and mercantile interests became more important for the state[14] (though her real non-aristocratic name Poisson, the French word for fish, inspired ridicule). Bourgeois merchants were able since the previous century leading up to the revolution to buy titles, known as *venal office*, in exchange for immunity from certain taxation which French aristocrats did not have to pay. Nobility already appeared as business, and business already appeared as nobility. Of course the contradictions in such a system and the financial depletion of state coffers from all the tax exemptions given to the bourgeoisie partly contributed to the French Revolution.

Political and legal developments mirrored technological and structural ones. The historical period of industrialization from the late 18th Century and early 19th Century onwards was both a political and a technological-scientific evolution. The two were deeply intertwined. There were singular events, but the overall trend towards industrial capitalism was a gradual development first in Britain and then around the world beyond Europe. The political side of it was the creation of joint stock companies, the enclosure movement, and the development of limited liability, etc.[15] These political developments and their social effects occurred alongside the invention of new technologies such as the steam engine and others which revolutionized the physical capacity of the economy to transform the raw materials of the Earth into economic commodities.

The law created incentives for private profit and expropriation exactly when the technology to make this possible developed. The end result of this synthesis supercharged growth starting at the end of the 18th Century in Great Britain.[16] We can look at these developments as two different but overlapping trends. Technology in itself hardly created capitalism since in order to have exploited technology in the way it did capitalism required a certain set of incentives. The technological capacity to create development is always matched by a social capacity to sanction development of new industry in capitalism.

There is an incentive to make money and the technological capacity to make products that make money which fuse together in the Industrial Revolution. The same situation which happened at the beginning of the Industrial Revolution can be seen repeating itself today, but with the 21st Century's current phase of technological development. The structure of incentives which we impose on the current phase of capitalism will determine whether we can direct technology in a more socially useful direction than how it has been used before. If capitalism could have evolved to the point it finds itself at now, then the economy will continue to evolve further. This is not the *End of History*.

Economic Exchange

At the heart of capitalist economic exchange lies the contract. A contract is the basic promise that a person will honor agreements made with other people. These give economic exchange the force of law, and thus sanction by society. Contracts are at the heart of the economic system of *bargains for exchange* that drives capitalism. As such the contract is a key structure underlying economic relations, and thus a key place for an economic reform to occur.

However, not all contracts ever made even in the status quo are considered just because they are properly assented to. Not all contracts even have the force of law because they are mutually assented to either. The contract has not simply existed set in stone since the beginning of history either, or even since the beginning of capitalism.

Some very fundamental areas of contracts have changed since the beginning of capitalism. The most obvious historical example is the legality of exchanges based unjustly on *slavery*. The slave trade of course played an important part in international trade in early capitalism until the 19th Century. Slaves provided labor in early capitalism. At the beginning of the capitalist era, human beings could also be considered property. This was not that long ago. An entire racist order established itself in the Atlantic world affected by slavery to sustain this exploitation which is still reflected in the economy today.

Slaves were dehumanizingly held both as a capital unit that could be owned and traded and also as a source of labor. Not again until today's robots, which etymologically derive their name from a word for serfs as we have seen, was labor again so explicitly owned.

Law is what determines what people can and cannot claim as recognized property. The law and the influence of ethical thought on it changes over time.

As a form of property, slavery, among other categories of ownership considered unjust, is seen as illegitimate now. Enslavement of human beings violates the principles of natural law guiding the universal moral framework, which of course was known from the beginning. Resistance to it on moral grounds was always present.[17]

Consciousness spread that slavery violated the basic premise that all humans are endowed with fundamental rights of life and liberty. Buying and selling slaves, once considered legitimate and permissible in many countries, now yields the moral condemnation of society and the law everywhere. This moral evolution eventually became expressed in customary international law as well as the laws of property and contact and fundamental constitutional law. Following the disastrous American Civil War – the United States Congress passed the 13th Amendment which states that: "Neither slavery nor involuntary servitude, except as a punishment for crime whereof the party shall have been duly convicted, shall exist within the United States, or any place subject to their jurisdiction."

The Thirteenth Amendment effectively banned slavery as a form of economic relations. The eradication of slavery on plantations followed the legal end of slavery. Gradually, slavery and its successors have receded out of economic life. Although the incentives to exploit other people survived as did sharecropping and other forms of explicit coercion, the legal avenue to make people property became harder.

Even in a fundamental area of economic activity like

contracts there exists *reformation* of the laws of society through history which changes the economy as ethical thought evolves. The question of what labor conditions are accepted by the law was never limited to plantations.

Feudal contracts and serfdom of course also formed a pervasive economic arrangement that gradually disappeared. In Russia a form of serfdom survived until the mid-19th Century. In both cases these disappeared not because they were no longer feasible in a technical sense, but because they were no longer considered just or even useful for society. They were no longer tolerated by the people – and it is the people who maintain the legal code through social relations and the government.

Feudalism withered away as the masses of people who toiled under its social relations defied it, as it became useless to its own productive aims, and then as it was rejected by the universal ethical framework of societies. People sought legal refuge in towns from feudal contract and the Black Death undid its utility. The institution collapsed.

The current arrangement of capitalist political economy could just as well follow feudalism. Ecological crisis will perhaps make humans choose between capitalist extraction and the planet.

Early American history provides examples of conflict in political economy that grew between different jurisdictions with completely different legal standards regarding slavery. Eventually abolitionism grew as a social movement and free states began to overwhelm the slave states until the cataclysmic break of the Civil War. The outcome of the Civil War was partially determined by industrialism and the superior utility of the North's free labor. Like feudalism before it plantation slavery went away. It legally disappeared in one jurisdiction after another until it was no more. Exploitation was at least diverted by a great legal and moral economic change.

What was a slave's human rights to a legal venue that did not recognize slavery?[18] There are many examples of this moral and historical question from history as well as literature and culture – take the example depicted in Stephen Spielberg's film *Amistad*. This is based on the dramatic events of the Amistad slave revolt and the subsequent legal case *United States v. The Amistad* that like the infamous *Dred Scott* decision dealt with the legality of slaves as property.

Based on the true story of the revolt on the Spanish ship *La Amistad*, in the Spielberg movie a slave revolt incapacitates the Spanish vessel carrying enslaved Mende people off the coast of Cuba. The leader Cinqué demands to be returned to Africa, but, unbeknownst to the captives, the Spanish navigators who survived took the ship North until it was intercepted by the United States Coast Guard near Long Island. Eventually the ship arrived on shore in Connecticut.

A trial ensues where the facts of the enslaved people's illegal capture are considered. According to the laws of the United States at the time, the slave trade was illegal. Slaves were therefore not considered to be a legitimate form of property if they were abducted from Africa.[19] The law of the United States and its international obligations with Great Britain under the Treaty of Ghent to put down the slave trade weighed against the claims that enslaved people were property under Spanish law. Cinqué is placed in a legal grey area between being a free human being, recognized in his inalienable right to liberty as free people would be under the Constitution of the United States, and being a commodity. The natural law of inalienable human rights eventually asserts itself. In the Spielberg movie, in a dramatic affirmation of his own humanity, Cinqué stands up in the middle of trial and shouts for his freedom. Eventually, Cinqué, represented by former American President John Quincy Adams, wins his legal case in front of the Supreme Court of the United States and is freed. Miraculously, he then returns to Africa. Unfortunately this case was followed by the United States Supreme Court's infamous *Dred Scott* case entrenching enslaved people as property before the American Civil War.

So what is 'legitimate' property and what equates to something like slavery? The answer to the question is not so obvious as many might like to think. Current sensibilities may have changed enough that slavery is no longer considered a morally or legally acceptable form of property, but even in the modern era there is a hold out of the legacy of the African slave trade.

In Mauritania slavery was legally abolished only in 1981. Modern slavery in Mauritania still has not ended though and is only gradually being eliminated. Only since 2007 could slave holders be prosecuted and it is still estimated that at least 4% of the population are still slaves in the very socially formal sense in Mauritania.[20] Less official though still de facto forms of slavery continue to exist as an institution in pockets all around the world such as in Dubai where Filipino and South Asian workers often toil without their passports under appalling conditions without recourse from the state.

If slavery has only gradually become considered an unacceptable form of property and is considered obviously unethical, then this begs the question what other forms of property are similarly illegitimate in light of newly enlightened sensibilities? If it was once somehow unclear whether human beings could be held as property and we now recognize it as obvious that they cannot be property, then certainly other things which are currently considered private property might not be philosophically justifiable. The boundaries of private property are properly just this – a philosophical and ethical question.

So this challenge of what *can* and what *cannot* be legitimately held as property is far from natural and easily settled, as some theorists of the market might contend; it is instead *the most basic question in political economy.*

Abolitionists argued that slaves, as a form of property, were being held in violation of an important moral side constraint – *that human beings cannot be considered property.* This is because being human grants people inviolable human rights which no person, law, or government can legitimately abridge. As Frederick Douglass declared, "justice, liberty and humanity were "final;" not slavery and oppression."[21]

This is the basis of the Enlightenment's philosophy of human rights which underlies many of the assumptions both of the economics of Adam Smith as much as the politics of Jean Jacques Rousseau and the other theorists of Democracy.

What is considered property is, in fact, a moral question. It is a deep moral question. What are considered legitimate practices of trade is a moral question as well. As democracy, human rights, and liberty evolve, more *jus cogens* rights will surely emerge. Many of these could deal with contracts that, like feudalism, slavery, or indentured servitude, are fundamentally unconscionable because they limit the liberty of the party with the least bargaining power or that of someone else.

An extreme form of capitalism stands not that far from indentured servitude or feudal contract where, as has been the case before, a corporate monopoly runs a company town as their own private estate. No practical 'freedom of contract' can exist where this is the only employer paying workers in vouchers that can only be redeemed at the company store for exorbitantly priced goods set by the corporation.

History has shown us that it is possible to wipe out a fundamentally unjust system of economic relations, and even to do it through a legal and political change in a relatively short period of time. By altering the legal form of property, the law can instantly affect massive amounts of value, and thereby permanently change economic incentives. This is what happened very dramatically in the United States after the American Civil War.

As Thomas Piketty has shown, the total value of slaves in the American South was substantial as a percentage of Southern American capital.[22] While he notices that the build up of capital stock measured in years of output in the Northern United States was substantially lower than in Europe in the 19th Century, to which he attributes the democratic character and social mobility widely attributed to it at the time as described by Alexis de Tocqueville in *Democracy in America*, in the South it was precisely slavery which made its economic character different than the North. Massive amounts of capital were held in slaves, enough to shape the entire macroeconomic character of the Southern United States. This should be fairly obvious just from a cursory historical understanding of how slavery was embedded in Southern life before the Civil War.

After the passage of the 13th Amendment to the United States Constitution, a formal legal change after the American Civil War, this economic reality changed since holding this type of property became deemed unconstitutional. The effect was swift, and immediate. Slaves no longer counted as a form of property. Slave owners lost their ownership rights over people without compensation, and the build up of capital in slaves disappeared. The United States legally expropriated the slave owners (considering the later rhetoric towards Marxism the effect of this expropriation of slaveholders is underappreciated as probably the most significant event in American economic history). An illegitimate form of property was no more. Obviously, no physical resources were changed by the passage of the 13th Amendment, but a massive change in resource accounting resulted along with a swift change in social relations.

The effect was obvious. Once slaves no longer counted as a form of capital, demand for them went away. Even if slave owners wanted to continue to hold slaves, they could not practically do so without the legal sanction for it. After the end of slavery when there was no longer any law protecting the old slave owners' property rights over other people, if the owner tried to clandestinely keep his slaves, in violation of the 13th Amendment, they would have no economic value to him in a court of law. If they ran away, no law could be called on to enforce his right to hold them as property.

Private property not considered to be legitimate is unable to be defended in a court, and this can fairly effectively prevent people from acquiring it. Without the legal apparatus of slave codes, property laws, and the power of the state to enforce them, the property regime that enabled slavery could not be enforced. Slavery could not easily continue after this.

Natural law prevailed. Without the legal recognition that slaves could be property, slave owners thence no longer had any incentive to purchase a slave. They had to turn to other means if they wanted to clandestinely continue a semblance of the Southern plantation economy as before. Unfortunately, this happened of course with institutions like sharecropping and prison labor excluded by the 13th Amendment. This was much less efficient and effective though than owning slaves. Outright slavery was no longer possible without legal sanction and slavery in its old form in the South did disappear. People could no longer be legally considered property.

Legitimate property interests change over time. Society has to come together and act to protect private property interests as a collective. These interests are not those which could be defended by one property owner individually against the whole world if society did not consent to help protect it. As Rousseau explored, the build up of private property thus seems to violate aspects of fundamental natural law, to which society has admitted exceptions since the beginning of civilization in the name of utility. John Locke as well considered it clear enough that starting out the Earth "be common to all men."[23] Private property would seem to be a massive exception to this natural order. The institution of private property, besides leading to all sorts of other concentrations of power, has evolved over time into more abstract notions of property asserted despite the increasing distance between the owner and the object owned. Could patent claims over a genetically modified organism bought from another person be considered truly justifiable property? If these property claims constitute a bridge too far we can still gradually claw back people's fundamental rights as we did with the ending of slavery.

We can imagine today a thought experiment in which we legally remove future rights of ownership over fossil fuels, for example, and consider what would happen to the demand for them. Engaging in a protracted campaign to regulate and tax fossil fuels could achieve a long term aim of eliminating them if done right, but it is also very complicated and removing the state's property rights guarantees for them *over time* could fairly seamlessly eliminate the role of fossil fuels in the economy. This could happen without the need to create a new form of regulatory state to enforce fossil fuel legislation or to create a new tax.　　　　`

Of course, it would be argued that fossil fuels are not such a simple category as slavery to justify a preemptory norm against owning them since they constitute no inherent human rights violation. It could also be argued that fossil fuels are still not entirely substitutable as a form of energy so there would be many practical considerations and a black market like with the drug trade.

Nevertheless, incentives to produce fossil fuels would plummet without a guarantee that contracts in oil or coal could be enforced. This would effectively sanction all oil. Finance for new exploration and drilling projects would become impossible. These extraction projects would not easily be hidden in a black market. This would eventually deteriorate the entire infrastructure around fossil fuel extraction until there was no practicable way to produce them anymore.

Such a drastic move, while very radical, should not be ruled out one day in the future on normative grounds. Fossil fuels create an obvious moral dilemma by causing the bulk of climate change that is not so dissimilar to slavery in the scale of its potential impacts.

A world without fossil fuels is growing closer anyhow. As alternative sources of energy gain a stronger position in the market, though not quickly, the possibilities for entirely substituting fossil fuels advance. Even today, certain countries have built up sufficient infrastructure for a post-fossil fuel world. Iceland derives almost 100% of energy comes from local geothermal sources while Denmark gains nearly 50% from wind energy[24] and as they approach a world without oil and gas this should show us what change is truly possible.

These Scandinavian countries will soon to be joined by others. Germany and the state of California among other large scale industrial economies have endeavored to create infrastructure to completely replace fossil fuels[25] and leave the shackles of oil behind – forever. Momentum is growing. The pace of climate change just demands that we accelerate this pace to avoid real disaster.

–

Choice

The law presumes that people come to arrangements about contractual relationships through free choice. In fact, choice is often the chosen paradigm in defense of capitalism as we now know it.[26]

Assuming the content of a contractual agreement is sanctioned by law, freedom of contract gives wide latitude to exchanges that would be considered unfair or unjust. When capitalist exchange is questioned, it is often said in its defense that people are 'free to choose' what they want, defined narrowly, despite the obvious fact that in capitalism, people do not always engage in economic activity to realize their choices or their will, but out of necessity. While people can of course bargain for themselves, since people need to engage in economic activity to survive not everyone comes to the table strictly out of their free desire either. It seems absurd to say that people are 'free to choose' what to contract for when wealth puts clear limits on what most people can buy which limits their real choices. It is an obvious illusion, no less than saying that people are 'free to choose' whether to fly through the air because some people could attach wings to their bodies and anyone could try waving their arms. Choice for capitalism is an illusion without the fiat of resources that enable people to choose. Choice requires the physical capacity of resources with which to make choices. There is no real choice without the ability to command the resources from which people are 'free to choose' which is the problem.

The matrix of choices on offer for people is limited. Inequality has only grown over time since the beginning of capitalism. Resource constraint conditions on what people can choose have grown. Choice in this sense is different from and should be distinguished from the political choice of what the system should be which structures the matrix of choices.

So, the problem and the question of small choices is really this – can people be free to choose when they do not have a choice to choose possible choices? Is this an "either, or" binary or a question of degree? In all fairness, can choices come to under constraint be considered as 'free' to the same degree as when choices are truly free of constraints? Here 'choice' when enforced *against* people starts to appear not so different from the 'choice' people had in feudal contract.[27]

The "freeness" of choice depends on the entire situation. There is something obviously false in considering a contract's terms and the heart's desire to be analogous. As well as the problem of *who* really has choice in the face of artificial, political resource constraints and *how free* it is, the other problem is determining *what* choices are legitimate – since not all choices chosen by the ones who choose them confer the same ability to choose to those people on the business end of this 'choice.'

Declaring all economic choices to be naturally legitimate ignores obvious harms to others, the topic of the entire discussion above, of what can legitimately be held as property and thus bargained for in a negotiation. Of course it is not fair or just to be able to 'choose' to own slaves. Today we can say confidently that we are not free to own slaves, because that violates the fundamental rights of those who would be slaves – not least the right to choose what they would do with their fate. This is a product of a *great choice* we have made. This was the choice we made as a world that slavery violated a pre-emptory norm of International Law and justice. This is the deeper issue with choice as we understand it. The scope and boundaries of choice is a political, philosophical issue.

The current economic-legal framework enshrines lesser

choice as the arbiter of what people want and what people do not want in a market economy. In the market demand makes no distinction between what is "chosen" freely and to what degree and what is compelled, or what is agreed to because it is simply necessary.

Modern notions of choice in this sense, particularly with consumption, cause anxiety. Philosopher Renata Salecl hypothesizes that the notion of choice seen in the capitalist market is largely an illusion as it is most commonly experienced on a familiar level. When we are bombarded with choices without distinctions as often we are the result is a situation where we are forced to endorse with our 'choice' at least as it is framed by ideology something which we really might not want.[28] Choice then is often used as a useful tool for forcing people to take responsibility for things they actually have no control over.

Choice, without distinction, is the critical feature of modern capitalist notions of consumption. As Henry Ford once famously said, "You can have any car you want, as long as it's black."[29] What a privilege it must be to not only get a black car, but to choose to get a black car from among all the other black cars!

The possible root anxiety of choice in situations that involve something more essential to life than a car is simple. Forced to formally endorse with 'choice' what is really someone else's choice, a person is not only made to agree to what someone else wants, but to also accept responsibility over it, to take it as their own, to swallow it.

This then of course provides a critical ideological defense to exploitation – 'yes people are miserable and treated unfairly, but look they chose it!' This ideological aspect of capitalism has strengthened over time as well. Since Henry

Ford's time of course cars have come in many different shades other than black. Now with the focus given to 'consumer choice' cars come in any color customers want – fuchsia, gold, etc. However, the principle remains the same as before. The dictum "you can have any color you want as long as it is black" remains. It has just been transferred to different types of choices as the system has evolved, particularly to large decisions. For firms the problem with choice is money. It is only rational for them to want to restrict the choices of those around them. Real choices cost money, which is what Henry Ford understood and why he wanted for a time to only sell his cars in black. In post-Fordism, with 'economies of scope,' the most obvious aesthetic limits of what car colors we can choose was lifted since it no longer would have any economic benefit to a firm, but the principle remains in force with other areas that still do cost firms money – working part time, vacation, and of course maternity leave.

We should notice what is really happening here. Choice, while free in theoretical terms in market economies, produces increasingly useless distinctions on its own if applied in a vacuum in the current matrix of decision making. While choice is supposedly enshrined as a function of free markets as well as democracy, increasingly people are given fewer and fewer choices about the big decisions involving the contours of their lives and the make up of the system, the sorts of choices democracies are supposed to enshrine with the people. The lack of real choice is reflected in the state of democracy. The real causes can be debated.

Looking at candidates for election in many liberal democracies, many voters increasingly comment that they "all look the same," that they are incarnations of the same philosophy, and that they represent the same interests. Whether this is true or not, and surely it is at least a very major oversimplification, the situation remains that the paradigm of "choice" has produced a situation unforeseen by the original theorists of liberalism. Amidst converging interests and a build up of power of those at the top, many people feel the quality of their choices is declining over time. Choice about which one of ten very similar brands of breakfast cereal to buy is the manner of choice given to people today when they are told they are 'free to choose.' To choose a job that will not pit someone between terrible working conditions and going hungry – too often this is not a choice on offer. To choose politically to reverse massive cuts to social benefits – impossible, not viable, all too often not something any party will commit to do.

Real choices remain few and far between and seem to be shrinking even as superficial 'choice' in the economy seems to be expanding, defined as more varieties of yogurt at the super market, or the excruciating choice of whether to get a car in purple, fuchsia, gold, or lime.

A number of successful business models help to show how empty the current notions of choice are for most people. Aldi for example profits on effectively eliminating useless choices while returning the efficiency of streamlined products to the customer, giving them competitive prices compared to their rivals.[30] The other stores' farcical dozen brands of the same cereal made by the same conglomerate to 'choose' from seem to not be missed.

The concentration of power in large corporations with vast influence over our lives is a choice society has never properly consented to. The real power this places in them is without justification.

To critique the notion of choice is necessary in order to reveal what people really would choose were they given a real choice. Choice in the economy made into a series of petty decisions, a tyranny of small decisions, follows a 'garden path' that leads many in a direction they never intended to go. Breaking large decisions into small malleable segments often creates this effect for corporations' benefit. Not that this is a reason to fear though. Real choices can be reclaimed through a consciousness of the political nature of the matrix of choices we are given.

What is missing is a *great choice*. This is the choice of what we want the world to look like – as a people and a planet – to consider the coordinates of a decision and whether these can and should be changed, not just looking at market choices in a vacuum as if ordained by nature. A great choice is a political choice. To make a great choice rationally requires thought and philosophical deliberation with time and debate on which course to take. It cannot be an impulsive choice. It requires logic applied to the functioning of the choice in order for the choice to be truly guided. Otherwise there is always the risk that a choice is really someone else's with the 'chooser' only used as a conduit and unwitting rubber stamp.

The 18th Century theorists did not see what choice would become, but as the world has evolved since then, the sets of choices on offer has markedly diverged.[31]

–

Ownership

Property is a function of the law. Its rules are defined by law as well. When they are enforced, they are enforced by the law. When they are changed, they are changed through law. Therefore, the law is the crucible of property.

Michael Hardt argues that private property currently seen as an exclusive monopoly of an owner can be alternatively seen as both a *bundle of rights* and as the *Common*.[32] The notion as private property as sole dominion over an object is traditional yet also a social construct. He quotes Hugo Grotius, "Ownership connotes something particularly one's own, to the exclusion of other parties," and then Blackstone, "There's nothing which so generally strikes the imagination and engages the affections of mankind as the right of property, or that sole and despotic dominium which one man claims and exercises over the external things of the world, in total exclusion of the right of any other individual in the universe."

He contrasts this idea of property to the Common, of "equal and open access" and "democratic decision making" along with a "mechanism to manage common goods" free of "monopoly of decision making."

A reformation of property could involve this sort of philosophical transition to *common property* – by changing what we could call property's *rules of engagement*, the fundamental legal relationship to property and the interplay and extent of the rights thereof? Michael Hardt has posited that private property can either be decreased by a reduction of what is considered private property, or it can be assimilated into an egalitarian program by distributing property more thoroughly among different people – something like the 'limited equity co-operatives' which he points out are supported by American progressive legal theorists.

The effects of this sort of change could be monumental. The creation of more limited equity co-operatives fuse ownership and use go together, for example, often through residence. Capital gains are generally limited to what one put in which could prevent the sorts of real estate speculation which drives up prices and inequality in cities, contributes to financial panic, and pushes people out of their houses. This is just an example of what an evolution in the law could effectively do.

Ownership, divided among the disparate members of society like in Michael Hardt's examples instead of concentrated in the hands of a few, could help both end displacement and help solve for the Crisis in Demand. This necessarily includes ownership of machines as well, whose yields help to generate inequality and concentrate wealth. Commonly necessary goods, products of objective demand, could be produced by society at scale to the point at which their relative value would decrease and their usefulness as a source of speculative profit would be low, like in the hypothetical example of the 'diamond machine'

With land and housing, this is much like Henry George's idea of common property. However, this same logic should apply to other areas of the economy as well. Ownership is largely today held in capitalist countries in shares of corporations divided quite unequally. These companies today control what Marx called the *means of production*. This includes the new machines critical to both our moment of crisis and the ensuing reform to our system. The law grants ownership to owners unconnected to the product of labor newly created by technology that produces without human input. This is not the situation foreseen by the theorists of the regime of private property.

.

With new technologies massive change alters society, and under the current law property owners assume all of the new added value created from technology *exclusively*. They will increasingly be able to replace hired labor with capital which they entirely own. This allows them to exercise complete dominion over the increased added value of technology. This is unlike past situations even during the Industrial Revolution in the 19th Century when factory owners absolutely needed to hire workers to run machines in their factories.

This means technology can potentially alter the basic and fundamental conditions of society and its economic ecosystem without society necessarily ever having a say over what happens or how – by transferring productive powers to owners which they would have previously bargained with workers to get. There needs to be a democratic debate about how this the effects of technology will be used and whether as a matter of law the product of technology should be able to be completely enclosed into private property as it has been.

This has to center on precisely the *legal* role of technology and how it affects property relations between people in society, but also where the boundaries of new forms of *private property* lie. For example, genetically modified organisms (GMOs), online copyright, and net neutrality all lie within the grey zone of expanded claims to private property that would not have made sense before new technologies made them possible.[33]

The idea that the holder of a GMO patent could 'own' (or at least be able to collect rent off of) every plant which naturally grows with DNA combined by a certain agribusiness should be terrifying. We certainly do not recognize someone who developed a new breed of dog as the 'owner' or even the patent holder of every subsequent dog ever born from that breed.

Effectively GMOs are no different from the end result of selective breeding. An important principle should be that the natural world cannot be owned. Biology cannot be owned. Life cannot be patented. Science labs that create new genetically modified crops are developing new breeds of crops just as agriculturalists have done for thousands of years since the dawn of civilization, creating new and better breeds of wheat or corn. Just because these are being made now in a science lab instead of a field, there is an illusion wrongly cognizable in the law that they must be like an inanimate invention instead of a new sort of biological organism like those humans have always bred. Before now the law never knew of crops that could be made in a lab.

This implicates the boundaries of private property. Many of the campaigners against GMOs for example have maintained that they are a health risk, but they have not so fully put front and center the intellectual property problems inherent in GMOs – that someone can lay claim to own the DNA of a crop.

It is impossible to fully deal with the effects of these issues in the economy without dealing with the problems created by private property. The encroachment of the rights of people by the claimed rights of property owners is the issue. As long as the products of technology are considered exclusively *private property* this and the further concentration of power into the hands of wealthiest will continue.

Like with other rights, perhaps *freedom of religion*, the right to property should also be balanced with a corresponding negative right – a *freedom from property*. This is

the freedom from having one's own liberty invaded by the
property claims of others. Technology only makes this more
apparent. Rights to property ownership should be conceived
as part of a package of rights that also includes the negative
freedom from illegitimate private ownership that impacts the
fundamental rights of the people.

Going back to what Henry George wrote in *Progress and
Poverty*, the law of property is probably the most fundamental,
and conceptually simplest way of changing the economy.[34]
Taxation and the particular details of state budgets are
complex topics, but the law of property is potentially simple
yet far reaching. A simple but drastic change in the law, like
ending slavery, can have immense consequences. Of course
those with the most to lose from such a legal change to
property, the most powerful interests in society, are loath to
consider it and will probably exhaust every other possible
option before considering changes to the rights and
obligations of such a basic law of capitalism.

Yet the problem we face really is in fact a legal
problem. If we take a look at climate change, for example, the
real problem creating the incentives for carbon emissions is
that proceeds of private property are fully enclosable in the
form of industrial production, but the 'externality,' that is the
emissions which are changing the atmosphere and
endangering the climate of the planet, are not.[35] Nobody
'owns' the harms of pollution and emissions. The same act
which creates goods which firms can sell for a profit also
creates the emissions which pollute the atmosphere. However,
the two consequences of this singular act are treated
differently under the current law.

Of course, this is an emergent problem of
modernization. Until recently, it was not even considered
relevant what sort of emissions came out of the smokestack of

a factory. It was seen as meaningless refuse that would diffuse in the atmosphere.

Like with the new emergent effects of a much larger economy, emissions are an emergent problem of scale. At a low enough scale, what comes out of a smokestack may indeed seem meaningless. It is of course theoretically possible to imagine a world without actually seeing it in which these emissions cause climate change, but without the new modern conditions which make this a relevant concern there was really never much of a reason to consider the possibility.

The law recognizes what can be owned and in so doing it effectively rewards and punishes behavior by defining what can and cannot be considered enclosable property. This powerful role of the law needs to be seen distinctly here from, perhaps, fiscal policy, or politics. Of course there should be good fiscal policy. This is the avenue for improving society which Krugman and others have proposed and which has been defended in the first section of this book. What the law represents though is the universal framework for defining the limits of property and commerce and perhaps even understanding it. This is the boundary of what can be legitimately owned and traded.

It is true, just as it was with slavery, that just because one country removes legality from a previously lucrative commodity, that other countries will not necessarily follow suit. The law can vary between nations, or regions, or cities, or even social groups. When the British abolished the slave trade in 1814, there is no doubt that this negatively affected their commerce as other countries such as Spain, France, or Portugal were able to move into the markets British ships were no longer in. Nonetheless, Britain, the 19th Century superpower, was able to control the slave trade and halt its expansion. Its hegemonic Royal Navy really did rule the waves including those upon which slave ships sailed and so Britain's ban on the slave trade mattered.[36] It changed the law and economics of trans-Atlantic slavery everywhere.

While no power now, not even the mighty United States, represents such a large part of the global economy as the British Empire did in the 19th Century, the United States and the European Union each represent around 25% of the world's economy.[37] China is not so far behind. Together, with a majority of global GDP, rules made by Europe and the United States can set the stage for the world's standards and with China they would be an overwhelming force. Even if we take the European Union acting alone, which presumably might have a serious incentive to cut into fossil fuel usage since none of its twenty-seven member states are net fossil fuel exporters, the effect of a change in the status of legal rights and obligations of fossil fuels would be huge. The law as a tool of broad economic change is potentially incredibly powerful.

–

Some Remedies

Here a path forward emerges, without specifying any one particular remedy for the economic situation we face. A number of changes, particularly concerning the laws surrounding economic activity, could help solve many of the greatest problems our world faces.

Property has been classified as *private property, collective property,* and *common property,* each of which should be seen in a unique light by the law in its own sort of sphere with a rational justification for why different ownership interests are governed as a particular type of property.

Old assumptions about economics have framed how we look at modern problems they were never suited for, but we can come up with a new and better economic paradigm. We need now to initiate this new era, a great reform of the venal and dated laws of capitalism that have remained in place for far too long. Many of the assumptions of the rights and obligations that constitute property generated by machines in particular can and should be turned on their head in light of new technical capabilities and new conditions.

—

Common Property

If we look at Henry George's insight about *common property*, it is that property owners, like Ricardian *landlords*, really make money on something that is not strictly theirs in a sense that can be easily philosophically justified, either through the appreciation of value on land or the collection of rent from their strategic position. They did not create their economic position, but merely hold occupancy over it. So it is irrational to treat them as if they did create it. This insight about *common property* was key to Henry George's analysis of economic inequality as he saw it in the 19th Century. What he meant by *common property* was the principle that the value of the Earth cannot really be owned, only used by people. Unlike private ownership of land which appears more like what Blackstone called the "despotic dominium," the landholders in his analysis of the 'single tax' would be considered mere holders of property instead of the sort of traditional owners of "despotic dominium."

Private property has been enshrined in the law over centuries. This does not mean we cannot change it though. "The Earth belongs to the living," Thomas Jefferson said.

Technological inventions have increased the power of machinery and production, the value of which accumulates to 'landlords' in ways which laws made in the past did not recognize. It is not just 'rent on land' that is not really the landlord's natural property, philosophically, but also as Marx pointed out the products of their machines which they sell but do not themselves create – surplus value, and as Piketty suggests, the fixed rents on capital investments. This is not to say that these rents and profits should never exist, as they can be justified by other means, but it is enough to say that they are *arbitrary*. They are a sort of wealth distinction which should only exist according to common utility, as understood by the French Revolution's *Déclaration des droits de l'homme et du citoyen*. This type of distinction is expanding in modern society rapidly since industrialization. As we have seen, both Henry George and David Ricardo knew that this was happening in the 19th Century. Karl Marx of course did as well. Inequality in Henry George's view was solvable in this way through law – by moving to a conception of mixed common property by imposing a universal and 'single' land value tax.[38]

That being said, as has been suggested, today the Georgist 'remedy' would have to go much further. In the 19th Century, Henry George could contend that land value was the singular and principal arbiter of value, with certain caveats. Marx certainly would have challenged the basic presumption that land and not industrial production was the engine of wealth in that era. Karl Marx was right about the primacy and power of industrial ownership owned by the 'bourgeoisie' as a source of wealth since factories with mighty machines have a huge impact on how the whole society functions, but this has progressed even further than he anticipated with the developments of automated robots that require no workers.

If we see 'land' in Henry George's work as a stand in for 'capital' most of what he suggests still holds true, so that *Progress and Poverty* still can provide an effective guide for how changes in the law could be directed. In this way, we should take Henry George's central idea, and philosophical framework, and pull it forward.

There needs to be a paradigm shift – instead of seeing land and capital as traditional private property, the "despotic dominium", to which we can do anything, we should see property as a *bundle of rights* that includes constraints and obligations as it had at its origins. There should be a formal distinction between *personal property*, and thus *private property*, and what would be *common property*. Property can have different rights associated with it, as it originally had in the sources of property law in the Middle Ages for some very different reasons relating to feudal tenure, that need not include an absolute right to enclose future profit. Property can have different forms.

The main objection to *common property* is usually the *tragedy of the commons*. The most common version relates to the propensity to work, which as we have shown is basically obsolete through technology while other incentives to do good things for the economy such as through services remain. The other *tragedy of the commons*, the waste of common resources, It supports *common* property to the extent that *common property* would remove the incentives for firms to overproduce goods which contribute to greenhouse gasses for example.[39]

As economist Elinor Ostrom has pointed out, many of the best ways of managing common resources are actually locally known and understood,[40] and often superior to a strictly private or government based approach. It follows from her insight that even a very expansive definition of *common property* need not lead to the tragedy of the commons in the way that it is seen by private property's supporters.

If there is a conceptual model here it is of a sort of shareholder society, an economic democracy, except that instead of becoming a shareholder through investing wealth, people become shareholders in society by the virtue of being part of it. This should intuitively make sense from the perspective of Enlightenment theories about rights. If we have reciprocal rights with the State in political matters, it should only make sense that we also have reciprocal rights in the economy as well. For example, if we submit, by agreement to a certain *social contract*, to the existence of *other people's private property* which creates inequality of wealth between some people who own property and others who do not, it would only make sense that the State, the arbiter of property, should also owe the individual a sort of social dividend, which they receive not from work but in return for their acknowledgment of property in general.

As Rousseau recognized, the problem with property to begin with is that the Earth has no natural fences, and all the ones we create are purely artificial. Since inequalities build up over time and become enshrined with property and then get passed on through the generations, the division of private property inevitably becomes arbitrary.[41] "Property is theft!" as it was taken to its logical conclusion by Proudhon. As part of a remedy for this original inequality, the theft from nature created by civilization, and as a solution to the economic crisis that hollows out people's natural sources of income, the universal wage has been proposed.

Just in 2016 the universal wage was put to a vote in Switzerland where it failed but still received over 20% of the vote.[42] An experimental version has been taking place in Finland. Such proposals have support from a number of leading technology leaders and even billionaires like Mark Zuckerberg who have put some thought into what technology's impact in the economy actually would entail.

Before the objection is made that this is a hopelessly ideological proposal, it has already been done. A version of this distributing oil revenues to citizens of Alaska already exists and was even passed by Sarah Palin.[43] A similar idea of a 'negative income tax' which people would get when they earn too little money was even discussed by Milton Friedman, not known as an exponent of social welfare.[44] This proposal is already fully in the mainstream and has had significant exposure already, for good reasons. It would simultaneously contribute to solving the demand crisis and the rampant inequality in society while overcoming the loss of jobs that will happen from technological automation. It is a very good idea. It would bring a certain amount of income into being as a common right.

Similarly Henry George's proposal from *Progress and Poverty* in 1879 to recognize all real property as common property would establish a general right to a certain amount of the commons in land that the wealthy that could not take away for arbitrary reasons – or hold market power over for the benefit of fellow millionaires and billionaires.

The common property 'single tax' of Henry George could open up property to ordinary people who might not have resources already built up in capitalism. It does this through reducing the monopoly power landowners can exert to charge money on the value of their land and drive up the price of living in society for everyone. It could shape co-operation for the benefit of all in a market, the end of Adam Smith's we should strive to create without changing decisions individuals make with the property rights that they do have. Holdings strategic land acts as a sort of private tax on the rest of society which Henry George's single tax remedies.

–

Co-operatives

Another avenue for *economic reformation* is cooperatives. The law governing co-operatives as a business entity distinct from a traditional corporation could evolve. Co-operatives are recognized as a separate type of legal entity in some jurisdictions but could further develop. Why have co-operatives not had a stronger effect on the economy?

Noam Chomsky suggests that many of the solutions to capitalism are in fact obvious and only require action to put them into practice and this is mostly right.[45] Co-operatives, a firm run and owned jointly by its members, are one of these. There are successful models of co-operatives such as the Mondragon Co-operative in Spain and the Cleveland Evergreen Cooperatives in the United States. These models can and should be expanded to other areas, but these organizations do not function well under capitalist rules of the market that drive a very different logic from what works best in a co-operative.

They require superior management because they compete in a system against capitalist corporations which function with an acquisitive, competitive mindset necessary to achieve maximum profits for shareholders. The leaders of co-operatives, on the other hand, rightfully are more likely to value the most immediately useful needs of their community and often have balanced interests rather than just pure profit. In a capitalist system though where profit equates to power, this is not the most ideal model for expansion of market share. With more profitable places for finance and innovative leadership to go, these co-operatives are usually the product of a sustained political project, and this is largely why they have had problems with scalability. For an entire area's economy to be run by co-operatives, they have to be generally attractive to the apolitical classes, and they have to be able to have access to finance, and this requires a large movement or the force of law to normalize changes to co-operatives' economic role.

No wonder it is then that the largest and most successful co-operative is in Spain and was a product of the Socialist-Anarchist rule during the Spanish Civil War. It organized largely in a capitalist vacuum without pressure from the typical firms that thrive in a 'bourgeois' capitalist economy. So for co-operatives to best thrive there needs to have already been a radical shift in the economic legal structure at which point large co-operatives would appear naturally much as businesses do in a capitalist market economy today. Creating this change is then part of the *political* question. So, much like the example of Piketty's global financial transactions tax, the moment co-operatives take over the whole economy is in effect the moment the problem has already been solved.

This should not suggest that co-operatives cannot be the chosen alternative to the multi-national corporation. Some sort of democratic management structure in economic organizations is desperately necessary.

A complex patchwork of economic business models is desirable and healthy for the evolution of society. There should be many configurations of work each with its own set of legal protections to maximize the diversity of alternatives available to each individual. Each should incorporate different aspects of socially efficient production and economic egalitarianism.

Firms too should have many structures of incentives to make use of as many resources as socially efficiently as possible. For example, in energy, firms should have reason to capture as many types of energy as possible, finding and capturing locally abundant resources, such as wind in coastal areas, solar in deserts, geothermal where there is volcanic activity, etc. Economies of scale can be established where possible such as massive solar towers which can be built in the Mohave Desert or the Sahara, but without undercutting local comparative advantages. A legal structure is desirable that best incentivizes this.

-

Collective Property

Resources owned by the state, or society, as a form of *collective property* exist in every country on Earth. This is a logical first place to look in many ways to reform property since society already has a right to have a say over how *collective property* is handled. While in many countries the state manages social welfare, vital resources are often publicly held for good reasons too. The Swedish power company Vattenfall for example is entirely owned by the government of Sweden. The necessity of public ownership of certain strategic areas has become more apparent recently since events like the British nationalization of major banks after the 2007 Financial Crisis. Also in Britain there has been recent talk of renationalizing the railways which has much support. Under the current ideological lens, state ownership of firms is seen as suspect. However, there are many examples where this could give a huge benefit to society, particularly in industries where there is a high potential for natural monopoly or perverse incentive. State ownership is not a panacea, but it should be a tool in the toolbox to find solutions to our economic and ecological crisis.

Public ownership opens up the possibility of creating a new democratic mandate over certain resources. This could be in the form of a separate elected legislature which solely determines the uses of publicly held land and resources and allocates it in the most socially useful way for everyone and all of society. This would add a degree of democratic accountability to any collective property managed through a democratic state. To ensure the better functioning of all state resources and avoid a replication of the capitalist corporate governance structure, there should be a further movement for transparent governance over state assets while reducing the influence of bureaucracy over public decision making.

Shareholding

A more radical, but entirely necessary path should also be taken to further change in the structure of the corporation. The most radical and direct solution to the problem with advanced technology, particularly how society decides how to use it, is to make the people into its shareholders – a system of legally established capital shareholding over powerful new technologies to distribute its ownership throughout society and among the people.

There should be some sort of *democratic project* for ownership which regulates how these resources are governed. It must address the new power created by emergent technology, particularly with automation.

The expansion of *common property* is potentially far reaching in its effects, as has been discussed. Its relationship with *private property* needs to be defined. The limits of what can be fenced in to create *private property* are always a matter of rational decision making and of great importance and the will to change them for a new era is critical, lest we find one day that property owns us.

We should turn the most basic assumption about the nature of property interests on its head when it comes to industrial production enabled by new automated technology and machines. The essential knowledge to create automated production should be seen as *common property* which private interests make use of. We should see the products of automated machines, industrial capital that incorporates labor saving technology or artificial intelligence, like the value of land for Henry George, as fundamentally *common property* which industrial interests are licensing to use from their factories' production. The products of these machines and the technology which creates them needs to be seen as *common property* for which society has a stake and an interest in seeing its benefits distributed as widely as possible. Knowledge and the products of self-operating machines, like land in Henry George's thought, have no natural rational justification for being fenced and claimed by any owner and so claims of ownership should be subjected to the same philosophical scrutiny that Georgist land or any other *common property* would receive for being used for private gain.

While a tax on industrial machines might work as well as the Georgist land value tax, the people as citizen shareholders of industry could work better. A certain requirement that a portion of the value of highly productive machines should be held by society and distributed among people in an equitable manner like a universal income assures that whatever would be the fate of the machines would benefit the people as well. It would provide society with a sort of independent 'universal income' separate from any tax transfers or universal income guarantees by the state. Thus, this would be the most fair and just way of distributing the benefits of technology among society – since the extra value created by autonomous machines, created by the machine itself, is not justly enclosable for one person or group at the expense of others.

Returning to the example of slavery from before helps us understand another way to return to the *Common*. When too much is enclosed without justifiable reason for enclosure, then there can be a gradual return to the *Common* through removing and restricting legal rights derived from the private property's *universal dominium* that has often categorized ownership. The human spirit cannot be owned, and neither can many other things. By vacating all claims of ownership over certain types of goods, society can maintain a distinction between what is just and unjust economic activity. Like with the example of fossil fuels given before, this could remove the incentive to build up ownership of property which is socially harmful or which is owned at the expense of others' rights.

In the reality of today, the law needs to recognize different conditions of society never before seen by granting different levels of ownership corresponding with different rights and different reciprocal obligations. The problem with the current conception of private property is that it is too one-dimensional in its view of what rights and obligations come with ownership. A more nuanced arrangement is needed to adapt to our current condition. The *common* ownership of the Earth can be recognized while establishing the principle that different aspects of personal, private, and collective ownership confer different relationships with society and different reciprocal obligations. This has historical precedent. Reciprocity of obligations for social utility is essential for just property. In feudal contracts, the *liege* was not merely the owner of his *demesnes* and master of his *vassals* but owed certain duties of protection to them and certain obligations in return for ownership over lands. This idea of reciprocity already exists in law, it just has to be updated and brought forward into the current reality. This principle might go some way to creating a theoretical framework for eliminating carbon emissions if ecological imperatives were inextricably tied to ownership.

As technology increases the number of things which have prices capable of being reduced or eliminated, they can be gradually taken out of the private property sphere. For example, music which we are able to download now for free on the internet has no natural price which it tends to anymore. It is easily duplicable, as are many other things with the advent of new technologies. This does not bring its costs to zero. There is still the electricity cost associated with running a computer. Also there is a certain limit of file storage, though this has practically been obliterated by *Moore's Law* of advancing computer power over the last decades. The supply constraints have not reached zero, but yet they have reached the point at which it is more efficient to let online music flow freely than to charge based on copyright ownership over it.

Flipping the entire paradigm of ownership on its head, the main solution to the question of property rights with products like these transformed by technology is just to recognize the natural *common* state of ownership. Music online has in essence has already been transformed into a stage of *common property* since the restrictions on its exclusive use are no longer technically feasible.

If products are made at a large enough scale, or if they are duplicable enough, fences around them naturally break down. The 'market' and 'Socialist' positions here strangely – or really not so strangely – converge. With commodities which can be easily duplicated or made at sufficient scale the transition to a very full version of *common property* is not that difficult with technology, if we embrace the necessity of doing so. Under the assumptions of *common property*, technology is able to naturally fulfill its intended purpose of making life easier and increasing the amount of goods available while reducing the work and resources required to produce them.

Another limit on private property should be that many instances subject to a reasonable use principle as a side constraint on exclusive ownership. With industrial capital this could be particularly relevant. Industrial property which is capable of furnishing social utility be used for a useful intended purpose, or the exclusive use right of this property can collapse into a right for many people to use it as it was intended. A primary example of this has been with squats and takeovers of old abandoned factories by their workers after a firm has moved production to another country. Better than having factories sit abandoned after a certain period of time has elapsed, workers who reopen shops should have every right to do so. Property in violation of this use principle should have rights to its exclusivity of use collapse into a right of joint use.

We can abolish the privileges of modern property owning 'landlords' to act a sort of private, unaccountable, almost feudal aristocratic power – and tether the power of corporations to what is socially valuable.

The overall *paradigm* of the economy must change to address the undeniable conditions of the present. The particular details of this change – and the process of how to achieve it – is part of the *political* question which we can only hope societies will start to answer. More of the same is not an option. A better world is possible and of course with the reality of climate change a better world is necessary. A true *economic reformation*, while confronting honestly all of the difficult problems this creates, remains the only way forward.

Selected Bibliography

Brynjolfsson, Eric and McAfee, Andrew. *The Second Machine Age: Work, Progress, and Prosperity in a Time of Brilliant Technologies.* 2014.

von Böhm-Bawerk, Eugen. *Further Essays on Capital and Interest.* 1921.

Čapek, Karel. *Rossum's Universal Robots.* 1920.

Chang, Ha-Joon. *23 Things They Don't Tell You About Capitalism.* 2011.

Chomsky, Noam. "Noam Chomsky on the Mondragon Cooperatives and Workers' Councils." 1994. https://www.youtube.com/watch?v=L9sV6peQgUk.

Douglass, Frederick. "What to the Slave Is the Fourth of July?" Speech to the Ladies' Anti-Slavery Society. July 5, 1852.

Ford, Martin. *Rise of the Robots.* 2015.

Frey, Carl Benedikt and Osborne, Michael. *Technology at Work v2.0: The Future Is Not What It Used to Be.* Citi GPS: Global Perspectives and Solutions & University of Oxford. 2016.

Friedman, Milton. Interview with William F. Buckley Jr. 1968. https://www.youtube.com/watch?v=xtpgkX588nM.

George, Henry. *Progress and Poverty.* 1879.

Hobsbawn, Eric. *The Age of Revolution: Europe 1789–1848.* 1962.

Hardt, Michael. "Property Law and the Common." Lecture at The European Graduate School. 2015. http://www.youtube.com/watch?v=7VIcZtU1q9U.

Kalecki, Michał. "Political Aspects of Full Employment." *Political Quarterly*. 1943.

Kautsky, Karl. *Communism in Central Europe in the Time of the Reformation*. 1897.

Keynes, John Maynard. "Economic Possibilities for our Grandchildren." *The Nation and Athenaeum*. 1930.

Keynes, John Maynard. *General Theory of Employment, Interest, and Money*. 1936.

Klein, Naomi. *The Shock Doctrine: The Rise of Disaster Capitalism*. 2007.

Krugman, Paul. *End this Depression Now!* 2012.

von Mises, Ludwig. *Human Action: A Treatise on Economics*. 1949.

Marx, Karl. *Capital*. Volumes I-III. 1867-1894.

Marx, Karl. *The Communist Manifesto*. 1848.

Marx, Karl. *The German Ideology*. 1846. Subsequently published: 1932.

Ostrom, Elinor. *Governing the Commons: The Evolution of Institutions for Collective Action*. 1990.

Piketty, Thomas. *Capital in the Twenty-First Century*. 2014.

Quesnay, François. *Tableau Économique.* 1759.

Ricardo, David. *Principles of Political Economy and Taxation.* 1817.

Rousseau, Jean Jacques. *Discourse on the Origin and Basis of Inequality Among Men.* "Second Discourse." 1754.

Salecl, Renata. "Our Unhealthy Obsession with Choice." *Ted.* 2014.

Schor, Juliet. *Plentitude: The New Economics of True Wealth.* 2010.

Schwab, Klaus. *The Fourth Industrial Revolution.* 2016.

Smick, David. *The World Is Curved.* 2008.

Smith, Adam. *Wealth of Nations.* 1776.

Soros, George. *The Alchemy of Finance.* 1988.

Soros, George. *The Soros Lectures at the Central European University.* 2010.

Soros, George. *The Tragedy of the European Union: Disintegration or Revival?* 2014.

Stiglitz, Joseph. *Whither Socialism?* 1994.

Žižek, Slavoj. *Living in the End Times.* 2010.

Notes

For a full listing of notes and related content please see the website at www.theeconomicreformation.wordpress.com

www.ingramcontent.com/pod-product-compliance
Lightning Source LLC
Chambersburg PA
CBHW060247290526
45789CB00001B/225